A DAY IN THE LIFE OF

TOURETTE SYNDROME

BY

TROYE EVERS

ISBN: 1478299703
ISBN 13: 9781478299707
Library of Congress Control Number: 2012913543
CreateSpace, North Charleston, South Carolina
Cover illustration By Hillary Fisher-White
Author photo By Kala Mandrake

TABLE OF CONTENTS

FOREWORD
By Susan Conners MEd

This book is a compilation of real life stories from people of a variety of ages and places in life who have Tourette Syndrome (TS). As I read through each story, they were all so eerily similar but at the same time uniquely different for many reasons. I saw myself in many of these anecdotes. This book not only takes you through the many struggles of living with TS, the teasing, bullying, punishment, physical and emotional pain and embarrassment that all of these people have endured. More importantly, it educates the reader as to what TS really is which is not necessarily, what is portrayed in the media or commonly believed by the general public. These brave individuals have exposed the most painful times in their lives to help us all understand that TS is different for every person that has it and that TS is so much more than just the tics. We read tales of ADHD, OCD, and learning challenges, all of which can be very much a part of TS for people who have it. To me the most important message that this book passes on to its readers is that despite the pain this unique and very misunderstood disorder has caused them, they all have grown not only to accept their TS, but to actually embrace it. They have succeeded in life despite the disorder and have become stronger and much more empathetic people because of their unique struggles. It's a heart warming, upbeat, inspirational, but very importantly, an enlightening guide to this baffling disorder.

INTRODUCTION

The world of Tourette syndrome is a strange and very complex world. There is a lot that we do know about the syndrome, but even more that we don't. If you say the words Tourette syndrome to someone, the first thing they think is screaming profanity (coprolalia). It is approximately under 10% of people with Tourette syndrome that have coprolalia. Most common tics people with Tourette syndrome have are neck roll, neck twitching, shoulder rolling, humming sounds and throat clearing, and facial tics, including eye blinking. These are a few of the common tics, but the list goes on.

Approximately 1/100 people are diagnosed with Tourette syndrome and approximately 1000 people are diagnosed each year. These are the people that are actually diagnosed. There are still many people undiagnosed and receiving false diagnoses. In these days, there are syndromes or disorders for everything and new ones show up every day. Doctors spend a lot of time trying to keep educated, but there are still doctors that don't know enough to make a proper diagnosis.

With Tourette syndrome comes numerous underlying disorders. A person diagnosed with Tourette syndrome, may suffer from one of these, all of these, but also a chance of not experiencing any of them. A child, who might have Tourette syndrome, will usually start experiencing tics between seven years old to thirteen years old, but the underlying conditions can start much earlier and act as an early warning sign. Some of these disorders are ADD, ADHD, OCD, social anxiety disorder, anxiety disorder, anger disorder, oppositional defiant disorder, and more.

In this book, I will take you on a journey into seventeen people's lives with Tourette syndrome. These seventeen individuals from all over the world, and all walks of life, will go into detail about growing up with Tourette syndrome, and what it has made them today. This is their story, their words. From talking about daily bullying, teasing, mocking, and their fight for acceptance, they open up to the reader and explain how they conquered the fear of honesty, and became strong, confident members of society with a beautiful message.

Having Tourette syndrome can cause a lot of fear, confidence issues, and confusion, so to have everyone tell their story for the whole world to read takes a lot courage. I have a great deal of respect for everyone who has shared their story with me, and let me tell their story. It was an honor to work with everyone who participated in this book. All of these people let me into their lives and told me things that they haven't told anyone, all for the sake of you to read and learn. A majority of people with Tourette syndrome spend their lives trying to suppress their tics, which in a sense leads to suppressing who they are. With this being said, I am so appreciative for all of the participants letting me into their lives.

Being a part of the Tourette Syndrome Association and a writer, I have learned so much more about Tourette syndrome, but everyone in this book has taught me so much more. I've learned more about my tics, my OCD, my triggers, and myself. I've realized all of the little strange things I do are all part of my Tourette syndrome, and I'm not the only one who does it. I was able to see a bit of myself in everyone. As a person with Tourette syndrome, we struggle with understanding. We try to understand what's going on in our own body, and we struggle with others not understanding us. While everyone in this book has a similar story, our stories are also so different. Tourette syndrome affects us all in so many ways, and we have not been given an easy syndrome to live with. I would like to thank everyone who participated.

I hope everyone who reads this book, gets something out of it. If you have Tourette syndrome, I hope you learn something more about yourself, and if you don't have Tourette syndrome, I hope you understand a little more about the syndrome.

This book is not meant to be used as a medical reference, but an educational tool. If you feel you or someone you know might have Tourette syndrome, it is best to seek help of a medical professional, or neurologist.

Clara 1

"I battled a full-blown monster that seemed to be in control of me"

My name is Clara. I'm a fifteen-year-old student at Greendale High School in Greendale, Wisconsin. I was first diagnosed with Tourette syndrome in the beginning of third grade. I was eight years old. This was just the diagnosis; I started having tics when I was in first grade. My parents started noticing that I was frequently stuttering. This was believed to be the first known symptoms of my TS. Not knowing what was causing my perpetual stuttering, my parents had me work with a speech teacher for a majority of the year. The staff and faculty of the school came to the conclusion that I could possibly have a speech problem. Of course this was inaccurate, as it turned out that my stuttering somehow miraculously disappeared.

The true beginning signs of TS really came out in second and third grade. One of the beginner tics I experienced was a quite loud and vocal "BOP! BOP! BOP!" This was one of my very first vocal tics, along with a strange barking tic. Although my parents would tell me to stop, my tics always left them curious. This is the time they started seeking the help of doctors. They took me to a neurologist, who gave the diagnosis of Tourette syndrome. I was going through all these motor and vocal outbursts, but I didn't think twice about how I was doing it. I know it sounds bad, but at the time,

I didn't care as much as I probably should have. While in third grade and being diagnosed with a neurological disorder was like trying to understand geometry. I wasn't really sure what to think of my condition, I was fairly young and took things as they came at me. It was something I had to deal with as soon as it hit.

My mother always described me as an "unusual, hyper individual." I used to pace around the house with books in my arms, and the next second I would be rolling around on the floor. It was peculiar behavior for a nine-year-old, but it was that age in childhood, where anyone was a ball of energy. Unfortunately, this wasn't the case. The unusual collapsing was performed in the classroom as well. As if nothing happened, my mother would hoist me up and guide me out of the congested classroom. I now refer to these situations as "the falling tic," which I no longer do.

Shortly after my diagnosis, my friends became heavily informed about my TS. Most were confused, yet very curious about my condition. I received many questions from many of my friends. "Why do you do that? Do you take medication?" Some, however, thought it would just be easier to push me around for my differences. Of course, all friendships have their arguments and small fights, but with my condition, it was easier to let people "tease me" a little too much. I was so eager to make friends that I didn't mind if people pushed me to my limit. At the time, I didn't realize how much it was actually hurting me.

With all the bullying, it made my anxiety skyrocket. I started getting a lot of anxiety after my diagnosis because of the severity of my tics and the bullying. It eventually became hard because I became fed up with it and I was growing tired of the same old routine every day. I wasn't upset that this condition would be stuck with me forever; I was mainly concerned that the anxiety that came along with it would eventually take a number on me. My TS wore me out and I was afraid of what people would think about it. I was bullied consistently and it made me feel so anxious.

My parents were more involved with my condition than I was at this time, they were older and wiser. At the end of the year, we visited many of my teachers and went in depth about my condition. We then went on to go to all the classrooms and explain to my peers what TS was and why I did what I did. After making these visits, I had learned so much about my tics that I never thought I would know at such a young age. I didn't expect to have learned something so advanced.

When fourth grade came around, so did understanding. At this point in my childhood, I came to accept my condition and realize that it was part of me. I managed to visit my school psychologist during the day; together we set up a time and date for me to go around to each classroom in my school. In these visits, I informed my peers more about my condition, and explained that it definitely wasn't something to poke fun at someone for. It took all the courage I could gather in order to deliver this important announcement, and it would not have been possible without my guidance counselor and parents.

After informing my classmates more about my condition, they were more receptive and understanding. They were educated about something that they knew so little about, or something that was completely new to them. My tics seemed so out of the norm for kids this age, it was hard to control the giggles. Before visiting with the classes, I would be laughed at and made a complete joke by my peers. I would be mocked, but it was such a relief to educate them about my condition, because the mocking eventually stopped. It was worth every penny to be able to talk in front of my peers and speak of my complicated condition. Around this same time, we had an educator from New York's national TSA come and speak to my elementary school. Many middle school students came to observe the speech and were educated as well.

From third through fourth grade, I attended a Summer TS Camp in Illinois. It was fairly difficult and stressful since my TS had reached its highest peak at the time. Most of the urges I couldn't control were more severe during my time at the TS Camp. When it came to the end of camp, I was extremely exhausted! It was a pleasurable feeling to meet kids the same age as me with the same condition. It became overwhelming on me however because there was a lot going on at once. I wasn't quite old enough at the time to understand, and even more difficult on the lines of fitting in. The second time I visited the TS Camp in fourth grade, a film crew from England came to perform a documentary on children at the camp with TS. I went along with the shooting and I was filmed several times explaining to the producers what my "tics" were. The producers seemed to be more interested with what my tics were rather than how I coped with them. To this day, I would love to be a counselor at the camp. I thought it would be great to say that I used to visit the camp. It's amazing to think that I could easily relate and come to an understanding with most of the kids. I understand what most kids are going through because when I was there age, I battled a full-blown monster that seemed to be in control of me. I would like the kids to know that I'll always be there for them if they wish to speak out.

My parents were my biggest supporters. Besides the activism in the school, they were also working to educate my neighborhood. I've lived in a tiny neighborhood and my parents came up with the idea to hand out flyers on my street for those to be aware of my condition. Eventually, my whole neighborhood was aware of my condition and everyone seemed to accept one another.

With a condition as unique as mine, I don't expect to be clean of bullies. The worse incident was with a girl I originally met in the second grade. At first, she played the friendly character and was eager to become friends with me. I was at the point of wanting to make friends, not having much at the time. Unfortunately, this changed in the third grade. She became physically and emotionally abusive all because I was different. During the third and fourth grade, I experienced bullying as I never thought I would endure by this girl. I was called nasty names, names that I didn't even know at the time. Her parents were insensitive as well, and believed my TS was fake. Of course, I was diagnosed, making this statement untrue.

When I was in fourth grade, shockingly, the family moved on my block. Whenever I took a walk around the neighborhood, her parents would heavily mock me. It was horrible; not only did I have to deal with the bullying at school, I had to now deal with it at home. Whatever tic I would do at the time, they mock me just as hard. It made it difficult to take walks through my neighborhood without feeling victimized by these people. I came to realize how immature adults can be. The parents spat out anything they could to make me feel generally miserable. They would yell, "You faker!" I don't understand how these people can live with themselves, being so cruel and insensitive, especially to a child.

Eventually the daughter printed out a piece of paper and claimed it was a police document. She told me that she had called the police and that they had reassured that TS was fake. I was completely stunned when she told me this. How could something I have known so clearly be fake in some people's eyes? She demanded to see my prescription medication, because at the time it was more severe. This incident showed me the ignorance in the world. So many people have stepped in my life with negative views upon me. Most who didn't understand would deem it necessary to mock me and pull jokes out of their pockets. I, for one, dealt with the bullies until I reached a certain age. All of my bottled anger was released during my time in middle school where the bullying reached its downfall.

Now that I'm in high school, my TS still affects my daily life in several ways. It effects how I learn in school, and at times, I lose my focus. My consistent body jerking can be overwhelming to the point where I am lost in my lesson that a teacher is explaining. It's difficult to stay focused. When I'm taking a test, I tend to feel more anxiety than normal. This makes any test hard because I'm trying to maintain hard concentration. I keep thinking, if I can't focus on taking a test, it could affect my overall grade that I receive.

Homework is a different situation that can be accomplished without feeling to anxious. Throughout the years, I've been beyond thankful for those who have worked by my side. They have taught me how to feel comfortable in a learning environment, even though my condition can be overbearing at times. Now I'm in an IEP, which I consider very helpful. They have given me opportunities of time extension on homework and test.

I feel extremely thankful to have such understanding people in my life. All of my friends are aware of my condition and don't treat me any different from the others. Most of my friends think my tics are cute and playful, that or they simply acknowledge it as a sneeze or cough. Around my friends, I feel like I can be myself and not worry so much about my condition. However, in the school hallways I tend to try to hold back. I get nervous when I walk through the hall and pass people I don't know. I tend to feel shy and try to control my muscle spasms. I worry that with my TS, people who don't know me will think differently of me. I'm afraid that they'll only have time to judge the outside and not who I am as a person. I never like to be profiled for my condition, as I'm sure others wouldn't appreciate it either. Once I get home, I feel relieved to be able to let out my tics that I've held in for the entire day. My parents have become accustom to this daily ritual.

My tics start when I wake up, and are wide-awake until I go to sleep. I wake up and start with my body jerking, and leaning forward and cupping my hands. I believe my tics are more active at night because that is when I'm doing the most activities. I am exhausted but at the same time, I'm eager to do something with my friends. A big part of my day is to try to unwind. I normally come home and sit in front of my computer or listen to music. I love to sit at the computer listening to music and playing a game of Tetris. I just try to end my day fairly relaxed. I will call my friends or my boyfriend and talk to them to relax. I also have my certain rituals right before bed. All my doors, and shades need to be close, I think this is part of my OCD. I also have to jump in place one time in order for tomorrow to be a good day. If I forget to do any of these rituals, I feel as if the next day will be one to regret. At times when I'm in bed, it takes me a while for me to finally fall asleep because my tics are more active at night.

For seven years, I have been studying Japanese and it quickly stuck to me like glue. I began to watch Japanese cartoons in elementary school, which was the stepping block to my studies. As a way to study, I would listen to the characters and use the subtitles as translation. To this day, I'm heavily involved in self-teaching, since my school doesn't offer Japanese classes. I study from dictionaries, documents, and Rosetta Stone. This is one of my ways of relaxing. Since I'm self-taught in the Japanese culture, I have a dream to become an English teacher in Japan. I want my students to be able to achieve a similar dream of what I have followed. I'd like to become an inspiration, a mentor, and a teacher to someone studying overseas.

I'm not currently on any medication, because I don't believe in prescription drugs to be the solution to my disorder. I believe the activities that relax me are the most reliable drugs out there. This is only my perspective, others with the same condition could feel differently, but that's how I feel. I did try different medication when I was younger in a desperate hope to rid myself of my TS, but they just made me feel faint and discombobulated. I realized this was not the path for me. My boyfriend did a day's worth of research to find a natural way for me to cope with my TS. Eventually, he gave me three pages worth of herbs and remedies. I placed it under "medicine" because of its natural effects that could cope with muscle spasms. He recommended many of these herbal remedies and he explained that they would subdue my tics for a short while, but not cure them. Some natural herbs he mentioned were lady's slipper, passion flower, Saint John's wort, and lemon balm. All of these herbs have certain chemicals in their plant that can lower muscle spasms from occurring. The lady's slipper contains volatile oils, volatile acids, gallic acids, and inorganic salts. When used medically, it is used to treat muscle spasms. I found this to be unique research and I'm still in the process of gathering more information. Some of the herbs I mentioned also lower dopamine levels, which is good in my case. A person with TS tends to have high dopamine levels, which could trigger their tics.

I would like others to know that it isn't a time to give up. It is a time to grow stronger by finding the things you hold dear to yourself. I found something that gave me strength and I hardly thought of my TS. I am a normal high school student like anyone else. I want to be educated, I want to learn, and I want to enjoy my childhood, as I'm still young. I participate in theatre performances and study a language on my own without any classes. After getting into my first high school performance, I realized that not even my TS could affect what I love doing the most. Freshman year, I was the "First Witch" in the *Tragedy of Macbeth*. I was ecstatic to receive one of the supporting leads, especially at my age, which was considered a "rare occurrence" in our school theatre department. When I go on stage, I feel as if my TS has somehow been cured. I feel that when the spotlight hits me, I walk out on stage without TS. I feel like the stage is my temporary cure because it accepts me and naturally subdues my tics. I've always felt that I'd never be able to participate in theatre performance because of the severity of my TS. It turns out that if you try hard to accomplish something, it will float into the palm of your hand regardless of what kind of person you are.

I am fairly open about my TS. I feel it is necessary to make people aware of my condition. It doesn't always revolve around "swearing" and "spitting out cuss words." My TS is a medical condition that needs to be looked into more. I'm never afraid to approach new peers to let them know of my tics, in case they are unaware. My advocating is that there are plenty of students and adults who have TS, minus all the swearing and cussing. I hate to be profiled as a kid who swears derogatory words, because that isn't me. It's not most people with

TS. It's very difficult to be labeled as such. Therefore, I make sure I explain to people clearly that my TS is only something that takes up a small portion of my life.

I believe that my condition is simply a blessing. Without TS, I wouldn't be as strong of a person as I am today. My condition has made me a strong individual and gave me the ability to fight to become the person who I want to be. In order to become strong, I must face disappointment and rejection from my peers. I've faced everything in between and it's only made me stronger. I've learned that I'm perfect because I'm different. It may sound odd, but it's the truth. Because of my differences, I learned that I was also special and could accomplish anything beyond my imagination if I fought for it. Nothing can stand in my way; in order to accomplish something, you have to jump all the boundaries that are in your way.

Johanna 2

"My tics control me"

Hi, I'm Johanna. I'm eighteen years old and live with my parents in Lititz, Pennsylvania. I've had tics for as long as I can remember, but was diagnosed with tic disorder at thirteen years old, and then Tourette syndrome at the age of sixteen years old. My Tourette syndrome is pretty bad, some doctors say the worst case they have ever seen, but I still have aspirations. I would love to be a graphic artist when I grow up, and maybe work for Apple. I'd also love to be a mom one day.

It was pretty scary when I first started having these tics, I didn't know what was happening to my body. I tried my best to hide my tics, letting them out in my room, alone. I'd like to think growing up was pretty average for me; I went to school and fit in pretty well. I never had many friends but the ones I had are very accepting of my tics and they did what they could to help. I would have my moment, but for the most part, I would try to save them for when I got home. I tried not to lash out on people or in public.

I started having a lot of anxiety when I was around eleven. This was also the around the time we moved to Pennsylvania from New York. It didn't seem to be as hard for me as it turned out to be. We moved it and settled fine, and then I had to start school. That's when the anxiety came out. I had such anxiety about starting school that

I just didn't want to start at this new school. I didn't want to go, but I pushed myself to go. I ended spending a lot of time at the guidance consoler. I tried to adjust to the new school and acclimate myself to my new surroundings. I was always good in sports so I joined some of the teams. I was better than this one girl in sports, and instead of trying to be friend me, she turned her little gang on me. That's when all the bullying started. At first I wasn't really being bullied for my tics, I was more bullied for my Asperger's and being better at sports.

Over the next couple of years, the bulling grew, and I started being bullied by everyone. It got so bad in seventh grade that I ended up missing a hundred days of school out of a hundred and eighty, which was just a massive amount of school. I was bullied relentlessly by the kids and then I would start to lash out and tic more. I would kick and hit them back. It really impacted me, being constantly reminded that I was the weird kid, the different kid. It started to be a constant struggle that I wasn't ready to deal with.

For as long as I can remember, I've had little tics, but never really much, and nothing that would cause concern or give reason to seek professional help. I noticed my tics as far back as seven years old, but at around twelve, they started getting drastically worse. I started doing things like shaking back and forth until my neck would crack. This could end up lasting a long time if I wasn't able to crack it. I also started moving my shoulders back and forth and in and out of place, and making humming noises while jumping. As I started noticing the increase of tics, I would try hard to suppress them only to get home and have my tic explosions get even bigger. These explosions would end up keeping me up at night because I suppressed them throughout the day. This was a hard time for me because I still didn't know what was going on with body. One night, around

2:30 in the morning, I was letting out my usual tics. I realized I was doing things that I'd never done before. I was twitching uncontrollably. I was twitching and making noises completely out of my control. I went into my parents' room crying, saying I couldn't stop moving. It was around this time the concern did start, my parents sought the help of a doctor who diagnosed me with tic disorder, and I was put on Tenex.

About a year later, when I was thirteen years old, I received the official diagnosis of Tourette syndrome. Ever since that diagnosis, the doctors say I have the worst case they have ever seen. I kept getting passed around from doctor to doctor but no one was quite sure how to treat me. Every doctor would just put me on a new medication to try and help the tics, but it would always cause more side effects then actually help with the tics. We have even tried many different concoctions of natural medicine, again with no result. Now I take pain medication as needed because some of my tics are so painful and debilitating.

Around this same time, I was also diagnosed with Asperger's syndrome, which is a form of autism. I was trying very hard to work through my problems with my Asperger's, which affected my social abilities and skills. It was very hard for me to express how I felt. I would often have rage attacks, which has been tied to my TS but I'm sure is a mix of both the TS and Asperger's. These attacks went back as far as when I was two or three years old. I would always tell mother, "I don't want to be a bad kid, but I can't stop." The mix of the autism and TS that we didn't even know we had at the time just made me feel like a horrible kid. I didn't know what was wrong with me, and nobody else knew what was wrong either, so I just thought I was a bad kid. It was a bit of a relief to actually have a diagnosis and some type of explanation.

In eighth grade, I didn't miss as much school as the year before; I only missed sixty-eight days that year. I found comfort in helping a friend. He had developmental problems and had a mental level of a five-year-old. I would help him go around from class to class and help him out. Through the year, I ended up getting attached to him and his aide. Having him as a friend and helping him out really helped me get through the eighth grade.

The summer before ninth grade, I had a surgery that went wrong and I ended up starting the school year on crutches. Walking into school on crutches, talking funny, and still in the same classes as the same bullies, I had reached my limit. I went home and told my mother, "I'm never going back there!" I couldn't handle it anymore and I never went back. Since then, I have been in Cyber School. I am very fortunate I made this transition because my tics ended up getting even worse over time. I know there would be no way I would be able to function in a public school setting now. I would be on the floor or in my wheel chair and not be able to grasp any of the material. Now with home school I can go at my own pace. I don't have to deal with ignorance from others.

My parents have been great and always work with me. They saw the struggles I was going through in school and supported the move to home schooling. There's always been acceptance in my immediate family, but not always with the rest of my family. When my tics flared up to a severe, debilitating state, my aunt had told my mother it was the fakest thing she had ever seen and they should put me in a mental home. She also got my uncle to believe the same thing. This obviously made me very upset. They have now understood a bit more, but that doesn't mean the scars are healed for me.

I have dealt with a lot of ignorance; the outside world is pretty ignorant toward difference. Everybody knows I have TS at one glance, not that they know what TS is, but they know I have something. Various times, I've been made fun of for my TS. Whenever I leave the house, I am stared at, laughed at, or even mocked. One time I went to a restaurant across the street with my dad—it's the only restaurant we go to since all the employees know about my TS and don't bother me about it, but the customers are a different story. One day while eating, I was very vocal, yelling "toes" and making a "hup" noise. I tried my hardest to muffle the noises with a towel I carry around for this reason. There was a woman who kept on staring at me and giving me evil looks. The woman finally was fed up and slammed down the silverware and yelled, "Shhhh" in my face. It was so ignorant. I was so upset I started to cry. I ran out of the restaurant to our car and cried. My dad went to the woman to talk to her and tell her I had TS. He explained to her that what I was doing was uncontrollable and was not meant to offend anyone. She told him it was very disturbing and I shouldn't be there. She continued on her rant and my father just looked at her and said, "The damage has already been done." There's always going to be laughs, stares, and pointing.

Besides TS and Asperger's syndrome, I also have OCD, ADHD, and SPD. The OCD is not a huge issue, but it's there. I have a thing for even numbers; everything has to be even numbers. I also have to repeat my tic a certain amount of times. I get obsessed with people and things. There was one point I had a big obsession with Craigslist. I would buy things to trade them just to do it again. As for the SPD, I always need a lot of white noise, and minimal lights. I always need the blinds closed.

Dealing with my diagnosis was hard because I knew there was no cure. We tried several medication and treatments with no success or relief. I've tried all the standard medications used for TS and tic disorder. I've also tried Baclofen, which is used for Dystonia, and muscle tightening. We have tried every treatment recommended for tics with no success. Nothing has touched the tics. We also tried various treatments like biofeedback therapy, including CBIT. Nothing has ever worked.

One doctor I went to wanted me to go all out with my tics for thirty seconds to see if I could get a break after the thirty seconds was up. They timed me and I went on with extreme forced tics. When the timer went off, I was still ticcing. There was no break what so ever. I was so frustrated. The doctor asked if we could try this again at my house, and I agreed. We tried it again at my house and in one of my tics, I fell to the floor and hit my head against the wood on the sofa. I gave myself a concussion. After that, I was still ticcing, but now I had a major headache. We also tried morphing my tics, trying to morph them into something else. This also did not work after several attempts and sessions.

After these doctor visits, they wanted me to be involved in a genetic study for TS. They were looking for the gene that causes TS. I had to give blood, and getting blood drawn can be an issue with my tics. Every time I have to give blood, we usually have to have two people hold me down and another person to draw the blood. It's not a fun experience.

My tics are pretty constant throughout the day, and affects every aspect of it for the most part. I tic myself to sleep and wake up moving and making noises. In the morning, they are more subtle, but as I wake up, they become worse. My TS affects everything I do. I cannot do simple tasks, such as getting myself a glass of water. I have things called tic episodes that are so severe I'm on the floor and can't stand. These episodes involve violent punching, jerking, shaking, and much more that have resulted in injuries, such as concussions, broken hands, and popped and locked disks in my back which have left me paralyzed for up to a week. I can't be left home alone, I'm unable to drive, and I can't do things on my own without having someone who can handle my tics with me. It really affects my independence. I spend most of my time in a wheelchair due to the severity of my tics and my tic episodes.

I spend a lot of time worrying. I worry about my future. With no cure, what will my future look like? I worry about leaving the house and it is a daily struggle worrying about who is going to make fun of me, or who is going to make me feel like less of a person because of my disorder. I feel cursed in this body. It affects my daily life, and I struggle to live with it every day.

Whether TS is a hereditary disorder or not, I would never blame my parents. They have been nothing but supportive of me. Sometimes I do get depressed and question why they had to have a kid, but I don't mean it as an intentional "you did this to me" kind of thing. I cannot imagine what my life would be like without my parents. Having such a debilitating level of this disorder is a huge struggle for me, and my parents are always by my side. I'm eighteen years old and I must say it's quite embarrassing but my mother still has to bathe me, wash my hair, and sometimes feed me due to my tics. I cannot make myself dinner or carry my plate to the table. We use plastic utensils due to the fear of throwing them, and we don't use knives. It can be a little embarrassing when my mother has to feed me in public, but it is just something that I have to deal with. I rely on my mother for a lot and she needs to go with me everywhere. I'm just thankful for such a great support system. Because of my TS, there are many things I cannot do. I cannot walk much at all because the tics in my knees and hips cause me to fall and I have my tic episodes. There are many things that people take for granted, even sitting still.

I just try to take it day by day. My tics generally do not give me a break, not even for a few minutes. I try to focus on things to keep my mind of my tics. I spend a lot of time on the computer and playing my Xbox. When I'm on the computer, I'm usually researching things that I'm interested in to help focus my brain, hopefully helping my tics settle down. I'm also very involved in a Facebook group for people with TS. This group is a great support group for me. Usually by the end of the day, my tics are running strong and hopefully I get so exhausted from ticcing that I just pass out. Sometimes I have episodes late at night and my mom will give me two Benadryl to put me to sleep. I'm also an avid bowler; yes, I love bowling and it helps keep my mind off my tics.

I have to keep in mind the things that trigger my tics more. Stress and anxiety are big triggers—I'd say more anxiety—and definitely other people with TS. I usually set other people's tics off but they can sometimes trigger mine too, but I don't let that stop me from meeting other people with TS. I love meeting fellow ticcers. Exercise is also a big trigger, but I feel because I tic 24 hours a day that I have a pretty good exercise program already. I can't leave out excitement, which definitely sets me off. When I get overly excited, my tics go nuts. I really don't have much control over my tics; my tics control me.

I'm very open about my TS to those who would like to learn more about it. If you can't cure TS, then we should try to cure some ignorance. I just want people to know I'm just like everyone else. Just because I have this disorder that affects my life doesn't mean I need to be treated differently. I can't control my body, but I can control my mind. I want other people to accept me for who I am and not look at me as some kind of circus freak. I'm just me, Johanna.

Michelle 3

"Always try to see the glass as half full"

My name is Michelle. I'm twenty-four years old from Long island, New York. I was first diagnosed with Tourette syndrome when I was fourteen years old, my freshman year in high school, but my tics first started when I was in the seventh grade. It only started with an eye-blinking tic, and my parents took me to the doctor, but since it had not lasted a year yet, the doctor diagnosed me with tic disorder and I was told it would go away. I didn't freak out that much, yet.

I was the shy, quiet girl who never wanted attention drawn to herself, so by the time I was diagnosed in high school, I kept my life somewhat hush hush. I never told any of my peers that I had TS. The entire faculty knew and I was allowed to leave the room as needed. By this point, my tics had gotten quite severe. I had abusive tics, meaning I would harm others and myself. I broke bones, and had mild coprolalia, and I would scream a good two hundred times an hour. When I would have one of these tic attacks, I would just leave the classroom and the teachers never stopped me. I usually went down to the guidance counselors, where they kept a "Michelle" folder. Once in the guidance office I would scream and bite into a pillow. I don't remember how long they gave me, but they did give me a time limit to twitch. I would have to let out all my twitches within this certain time or be sent home for the day, and that drove me nuts. If I had to leave school, it would count as a missed day, which would affect my chance to graduate on time. I hated this, because it was something I had no control over. I didn't end up going home that much. I would just try to let my tics out for as long as they would give me and then suppress them the rest of the day. It was hell! I could not focus on anything except needing to twitch. When I got home, it would be a horror show, because I would just go off.

Ninety-five percent of my friends that I had growing up left me because I got too weird for them. I made many attempts to make new friends, but they didn't know how to deal with me. I did make some friends, but I soon realized they were only friends with me because I was older than they were and could buy, and do stuff for them that they could not do. With a condition like mine, I guess you do anything to fit in. Thankfully, now I know who my true friends are and that a few good ones are all you really need in life.

When I was looking for a college to attend, I was luckily enough to find one with a SASS department (Student Academic Support Services). It was great; this meant they would be willing to work with me instead of against me. I attended the school and got my degree in Social Work, because I love helping others. Since I went to college more than four hours away from home, they would help me if I got homesick, or felt something was wrong with my medication, or even if I just needed someone to cry to, especially after my nana passed away. They were very understanding to people with disabilities and did all they could do to help. I was allowed a separate testing room, and extra class time to take exams so I would not be as stressed. Sometimes I would not even use the accommodations, but just knowing I had them to fall back on made me more relaxed.

Even with the SASS, I did have some problems. My final semester in college, looking back at my transcript I realized that without trying I basically obtained a minor in psych but was just one class short. I took an open psych class that fit with my schedule so that I'd graduate with a minor in psych. The professor was...evil! She didn't believe in "special needs." She felt that everyone should learn the same way. I was basically penalized for having a "disability." She made my life hell even with the SASS. She always wrote her tests in a trickery form and if I asked for help understanding a question, she wouldn't read it to me because she felt I could do it on my own. If I would go to SASS and get help from them, she'd hold it against me. All through college I maintained a 3.4 GPA, but because of her, I graduated with a 2.8. She never gave me extra help, even thought I'd go to her. I did everything in my power but she thought I was faking. I *so* regret taking that class! You would think of all professors a psychology professor would be the most understanding.

Along with my tics, I have the package of underlying disorders too. I have ADD, OCD, anxiety disorder, depression, paranoia, and I get mood swings. My OCD is pretty bad. I have to wash my hair four and a half times in the shower, four real times and one real quick. I have to beep lock my car door four times in order to feel that it is really locked. When I do laundry, I have to hit each button on the washing machine four times to believe and feel that it is really working. Before I can leave the house, I also have to close my bedroom door against my foot nine times and then slam it before I'm able to leave the house.

When I was younger, about elementary age, I had OCD but was unaware it was OCD until I got my TS diagnosis. I would have to lock my front and back door for seven minutes each and then stare at both of them for seven minutes as well as the windows. I would then have to stand in my bedroom door and stare at both doors again for another seven minutes in order to feel totally safe and that the doors and windows were locked. I also had the "bug check" where I would look around every inch of my bedroom for a bug of any sort and if there was something, I'd have to wake my father up and he'd have to kill it. I would not be able to go to sleep until it was dead and out of my room.

Not everyone understands how frustrating it is to have no control over you own body and how sometimes you just lash out because it's what has to be done. Thankfully, as I've gotten older, my tics have gotten better and now on a "normal day" I just growl and blink. Even with that, it's still hard to be a twenty-four-year-old. It's hard for me to go out with friends and grab a drink. Some friends like to go out a grab a beer and go home, because to them, one beer doesn't seem to do anything, but I can never do that. With all the medication I'm on, I'm not able to have just one beer and drive. I get tipsy and drunk much faster than others do, which makes it annoying when friends want to just go and hang out. It's not like I like to drink a lot, but I would like to go have a social drink with friends. Sometimes I will go out, but I make sure not to take my medication that night, but I feel the effects. The next day I feel like a zombie for not having the medication in my system since I'm so immune to it.

It's also hard to date, and going out to the movie. If I go out to meet a guy that I'm interested in, I'm always down on myself, thinking he won't like me because I have TS. It's not an easy thing to discuss and explain. A majority of the population might be accepting of it, but it doesn't mean they understand it. I'm always afraid I'll never find someone to love and accept me for me and grow old together. I can go to the movies, but usually don't like to because when there is a quiet scene it's hard not to twitch and make some kind of noise. It's just hard for me to sit still for too long. This can also be an issue in a work setting. There is no way I could sit still for eight hours in a cubical, especially if there are people around. I don't know why, I'm just more twitchy and nervous around people.

When I was eighteen, I went into the city with my brother to see a Broadway show. I was having a bad twitchy day and didn't want to go, but decided to suck it up. As soon as we got on the Long Island railroad into the city, my tics got bad, so I called my friend to see if she wanted to take my place, but she couldn't. I sucked it up and went to the show. I suppressed my tics so hard that I was actually quiet through the whole show, but as soon as we came out it was a massive tic attack. I just couldn't stop "ticcing." My brother knows that I have TS, but had never been alone with me to see my tics so bad. We got onto the Long Island railroad to go back home. Apparently, I was not welcomed on that train; I was very ticcy, and doing my screaming tic. My screaming tic was like a horror movie murder scream, and quite loud. I was really bad from suppressing my tics for so long during the show, I just could not suppress anymore. I'm sure I was doing other tics, but all I can remember doing were the scream, snorting, and growling tics.

I was just having a tic attack and nobody even bothered to ask if I was okay, if I needed anything, or if I had a problem. Instead, while I'm ticcing, embarrassed, and in pain the entire train just hysterically laughed at me. It was like being on a train full of four year olds. My brother tried to calm me down and take my mind off it. I think he was worried about my coprolalia coming out. With my coprolalia, I would occasionally scream out the word "nigger." One guy on the train was extra aggravated by me and got out of his seat and threatened me for my life, this guy happened to be African American, which just made my brother nervous since he didn't know if I was going to scream out something offensive or not.

We didn't know this person, or anyone else on the train, but there were a few nice people. Some of them realized that I had a medical disorder and I could not help myself. They actually started yelling at the other people on the train to "shut up and leave her alone." People actually started fighting over whether or not I was just being immature, or actually did have a medical condition.

The train incident really messed me up for a while. I became afraid of trains. Whenever I would be at a railroad crossing, I would have to put my sun visor down to block the view and blast the radio to tune out the sound. Sometimes I'd get so freaked out I would turn on the first block I saw before I got to the track. One time I did this not realizing it was a one-way street, going the opposite way. About a year later, it took three close, and strong, friends to each carry a part of my crying and shaking body back onto a train for me to get over this fear.

When I was in high school and newly diagnosed, I did everything to keep my TS a secret. However, since college, living on my own, and certain experiences, I've become more open about it. My father was part of the Rotary, and because of the train incident, his Rotary club had thousands of disposable cards printed out. One side of the card said, "I'm sorry for startling you," and the other side explained that I have TS and what it is. Now, if someone gives me a dirty look or looks confused, I just hand them a card.

When I'm aggravated, stressed, tired, frustrated, or nervous, the tics are bad. It really triggers my tics. My triggers are not as bad as they used to be, but the main ones that would always set me off can still occasionally set me off. One of them is when someone says, "Shhh." I cannot be shhh'd! I would rather someone tell me to flat out "shut up." It's just how people say it in such a low voice that sets me off. I would go nuts when a teacher would "shhh" the class.

The word "goodnight" also used to set me off. If I was leaving a restaurant and the server or someone would say, "Bye, have a goodnight," I would go, "Goodnight, goodnight, goodnight, goodnight...." That set off my coprolalia. I would also do this thing with my dad where I'd say goodnight and he'd have to respond in a squeaky version and it had to be perfect or we'd have to keep doing it. I also had another trigger where if I saw the word "cock" I'd have to scream it. If it was written on the menu somewhere as a cocktail, I'd see it and have to scream. Most of the time I'd try to cover it up by adding to the end of the word and saying, "Cock-a-doodle-doo," or "Cock—tail" or something along those lines. Those were my three "main triggers." I'll still do these occasionally on a bad day, but it's rare. Now my main trigger is that you can't touch me, especially without warning. If you want to hug me or something you have to tell me and I'll brace myself for it but I can't be touched without warning.

I know to calm myself down I have to relax. I try to take a nap on the days that my tics are bad so I can relax. Try to calm myself down and rebuild myself up. I'll just put on a good TV show and lie down. What's really great to help me unwind is a massage. I love to go to the nail salon to get a back massage as much as I can; it relaxes me and brings down my tics.

I'd say, over all, I've dealt pretty well. I started going to local support groups from the beginning and always tried to see the glass half-full. I found the Long Island TSA support group, which has been a great help. I love everyone in it and am so thankful for it. I might start going to the NYC support meetings soon to meet people my own age. The more people the merrier. I've also found a bunch of TS friends through the national TSA Facebook page. Granted, I don't know them personally but we can still give each other advice on those bad days and be there for one another.

I'm thankful to have such amazing, loving, and understanding parents that stand up for me and advocate for me. They do their best to understand what I go through, since neither of them have TS. I could never blame them and would never trade them in.

I'm a big believer in you get what you can handle and I was given this because I can handle it. I try to look at it as a blessing as much as possible. I was given this for a reason, and I'm going to embrace it. There are so many people out in the world, and I'm glad to be different and stand out. I feel you meet better people this way and become a more caring individual to others.

I have Tourette syndrome, I'm not a monster, it's not contagious, and it's who I am. It's what makes me... me. Yes, I might make weird noises from time to time, but I'm still a person. I still have feelings; I cry like everyone else. I just want to be accepted. If someone has a question as to why I'm doing something, ask me. I won't hurt you; I want to educate you. Everyone has something, everyone!

Gary 4

"We roll with the punches"

I'm Gary, from the Big Apple, NYC. I'm twenty-five years old, born and raised in Rockland County. Although I had symptoms for years, I wasn't officially diagnosed with Tourette syndrome until I was eighteen years old, the summer before going into college. I had tics for as long as I can remember. I had a great supportive family, both my parents came from two very different backgrounds, but they made a point to raise all three of us kids with modesty, kindness, and kindness for other. I'm the youngest of three, and my parents just wanted the best for us.

My childhood was somewhat nerve wracking. Before I was diagnosed with TS, I was continually told that my anxiety developed when my father had some health problems when I was seven years old, but everyone thought it was something different. No one knew what it was, or what to do. If I had a tic with my stomach, I was sent to the gastroenterologist. If I had a tic of clearing my throat, I was sent to a speech pathologist. My general practitioner, who was my doctor since birth, had no idea why I was doing what I was doing. My mother, who was a special-ed teacher, wasn't even able to provide any type of answer.

When I was seven years old, my father's health started getting bad and that's when my tics really started. My father had a heart procedure, and then hurt his back. Over the next ten years, he ended up having another heart procedure and three back surgeries. This planted the seed of worry in me, which lead to the OCD of always being afraid of my father going to die. I wanted to do anything to prevent this. I was constantly biting my tongue and would say an old, ritualistic Jewish saying. If I said it twice, I would have to say it one more time, because I was afraid the second time canceled out the first one.

Around this time, I was diagnosed with ADD. I remember being in first grade and the teacher reading a book to the class, and I zoned out. When I came back, I thought, "Geez, where did the last few minutes go? I don't remember the story." My parents brought me to the doctor and I was put on Ritalin. Also around this time is when my motor tics started to appear. I had a strange and interesting tic. I had one tic where I would snap my head back as if I was trying to crack it. This tic made me look like I was walking like a pigeon because I couldn't stop. One time, when we were on vacation, my parents said, "Stop it! Enough is enough, just stop it."

Despite my new developing issues, my parents were always very supportive. With my OCDs growing, I started having issues with sleeping anywhere else except my own bed. I was at the age of kids having sleepovers. I was just unable to participate, but was embarrassed to tell my friends the reason why. My mother and I created a code; when a friend asked me to sleep over, I would ask her if I could, and she knew to say, "Not tonight." I would always put up a little fight, but she knew I really didn't want to go.

In eighth grade the blinking started. People would ask me what was wrong, but I didn't know. I had no idea what was going on so I would just come up with stories. Everyone started to think it was just an annoying habit. They'd comment, and some people would tease me, but I would just blame it on other things. If I was blinking, I would just say my contacts were dry, or I recently had some type of procedure. This is also the time that my throat-clearing tic started. Friends would make fun of me; they would mock and impersonate me.

By the time I got into high school, most of the tics calmed down a lot. I didn't really tic that much. This was a big relief and I thought whatever was wrong with me was gone. I had a good high school period. I played sports, tennis, and was involved in student council. Senior year things started getting bad again. I started blinking a lot again.

I was accepted into Cornel, my dream school. Right after my high school graduation, I got sick. Usually when I got sick, I would end up with strep throat. One day I told my father that this time was different and that I felt worse. At first, he just said to suck it up, but eventually we went to the doctor. The doctor said I had mono. This scared me, as I had no idea about mono except what you hear in school, where kids would miss out months of school and were bed ridden. I was scared that I wasn't going to be able to start college at the end of summer. I think because of the stress of having mono, and starting college, my tics all started getting worse. I was blinking, throat clearing, and pushing out my stomach more and more.

Through the summer, we sought out the help of other doctors one more time to try to figure out what was going on. We went to a doctor and he told my mother to wait in his office while he and I went into the examination room. I liked to bring my mother along, especially with first-time visits. She spent most of her life around doctors, and it was good to have a second set of ears around in case I missed something. The doctor did some basic tests: follow the light with my eye, reflex-reaction test. He finished up and we walked back to his office. I thought to myself, "Wow, I aced these tests!" We walked into his office and he sat down, looked at my mother, and said, "Your son has Tourette syndrome." That was the first time that that term was used in reference to me. I didn't know what exactly it was. I think at first I thought it was what the media stereotype had portrayed it to be, a bunch of vocal tics.

I didn't believe I had it, but when we got home, I went to my father and he asked how it went. I told him they said I had TS. He looked at me and said, "Shit ass fucker balls ass licker." I said, "Dad, it's not funny!" He repeated it again, and then saw the concern in my eyes. My life had changed forever. It was no longer a nervous tic. I had TS, and we knew I was going to be on a lot of medication. It wasn't from being stressed, or the mono. This was a neurological condition that I would always have. It's now medical. We knew we found out what was wrong, and now we had to deal with it. My family is supportive of each other, but at the same time, we joke about it. The way we see it, we roll with the punches. You have to be able to laugh at yourself.

I went to see a specialist doctor at NYU but before I was able to see the doctor, I had to meet with her assistant. That meeting really fucked me up. He asked me all these weird questions: "Have you ever considered suicide? Do you think of rape or murder or any violent behavior?" I guess it I was something that coincided with TS, but I felt weird being asked this. It's like telling someone not to think of a pink elephant; what are you thinking of now? A pink elephant.

After the official diagnosis, my mother called my general practitioner and told him. He felt really badly that he didn't catch on. My mother was also distraught because she didn't catch on. She didn't notice and felt she should of, being a special-ed teacher. She wasn't able to pin point the problem. She went on to dive into researching medication and more about the disorder.

As the summer ended, it was time to start thinking about starting Cornell. Cornell is a big fraternity school. I went early and tried out for a fraternity. Had to go up a week early before school started, which was hard with having mono. It's a big drinking week, and I couldn't drink. I didn't make the fraternity, but at least I was able to start college on time despite the mono. My tics were relatively bad, lots of blinking. I did make friends, but about two months into the first semester, one of my friends, a girl on my floor, admitted that, at first, they called me twitchy behind my back because of the blinking. I walked around confident; I tried to be my normal, charming self. She also said, though, that they found out I was actually a pretty cool guy and stopped. It just goes to show you that with TS, you often start at a disadvantage and you have to compensate for it; you have to do 125% to equal someone else's 85%.

After the first semester of school, I stayed at a friend's house during the break between semesters. One night I watched *The Butterfly Effect*. I needed to escape the new life (TS and school). Hell, it's Ashton Kutcher; how could this be scary? Something in the movie triggered something in me. I spent the rest of the night laying on my friend's futon, sweating, crying, and ticcing like crazy. By the time morning came and my friend woke up, I acted as if everything was okay and I left. Shortly after I left his house, I pulled the car over and started hysterically crying. I called my parents and told them I wanted to kill myself and I was very upset. I ended up going over to my parents for dinner then back to school. I was in a very dark place but I continued to push on and ended up graduating a semester early.

Right out of college, I started as a sales and marketing assistant at a big NYC hotel. One day when I was out with my boss at a wedding, he noticed my blinking and asked me if he made me nervous. I said no, and thought to myself, "Fuck it." I told him I had TS, explained it, and told him if he had any questions to feel free to ask. That was on a Saturday, by Tuesday, everyone in the hotel and coworkers knew I had TS. My boss would make jokes about it. If I were taking a group on a tour of the hotel, or the space, my boss would introduce me and say he has TS, so if he calls you a fucking shit hole, just ignore him. I was devastated. I felt very betrayed and I ended up leaving that job soon after.

Since then, I was wary, but I have told my bosses after a few months. I feel as if I have to, so I can explain the noises I make, and the meds I'm on. I'm consistently asked, "What are those noises you're making?" Sometimes I try to make an excuse, but for the most part, I try to be honest, it just depends on the situation. Most people thought it was minor enough, and my other qualities made up for it, but there were those people who treated me special as if I needed assistance to get things done.

After leaving that first job, I did a little job-hopping. I ended up seeking the help of a career coach because of the problems I was having with my bosses. Everyone, mainly my parents, came to the conclusion that I had a problem with authority and needed to suck it up. The career coach was a step in the right direction. She was great and helped me get my current job as a sales rep for a wine and liquor distributer. I live on the UWS of Manhattan and was assigned the territory of Queens and Long Island, so I had to drive. About a month after I started, I was hit by an eighteen-wheeler and totaled my car. I somehow was okay, minor injuries. It made me think of life in a different way. You can invest so much in your children and it can all be taken away in the blink of an eye. Driving now is one of my triggers. I get very ticcy and anxious, especially around trucks, but I have to drive for work, so I have to suck it up.

My tics are always changing, from blinking to breathing patterns, teeth grinding, etc. I have been through a lot of therapy to know what I have to do to calm down. Step back and breathe. I've been put on many medications. At one point I was on Abilify, but it caused me to gain weight. Now I'm on antidepressants, blood pressure medication (used for TS), Klonopin, vitamins, and ADD medications. I also take a medication to help me sleep. I'm unable to sleep in complete silence and darkness, my mind runs wild with thoughts. I usually fall asleep to my TV on a sleep timer. I know it sounds bad, but I somewhat feel cursed. I wish I didn't have to deal with the issues that have come along with TS.

I've experimented with alternative methods to helping my TS, too. I did hypnotherapy, which worked the first time for a few hours, then I thought about how I hadn't been ticcing, and I started ticcing again. I did the biofeedback, which just felt like an odd mental video game. Two things that I did feel that helped a lot were massage and acupuncture. Although expensive, I do find them to be relaxing.

I had heard of studies about marijuana used to relax and calm down tics. I have a neighbor who has MS and uses it to help him, so for a short while, I would smoke a few hits before bed each night. Half the time it relaxed me and made me calm, and half the time I would end up eating everything in my kitchen. Besides the munchies,

I think marijuana usually has a calming effect, but I have had bad experiences too.

I also deal with issues related to OCD, anxiety, and germaphobia. Growing up, it used to take me half an hour to lock up the house. I would have to re-check the locks, the doors, the garage door, alarm system, etc. Now I live in an apartment and my front doorknob is loose because I pull on it and twist it when locked to ensure it can't be opened. I also unplug the toaster oven, turn the knobs on the stove, and continuously touch the light switches in my apartment to ensure that no water or moisture from my hands will seep into the socket and start a fire.

I deal with many different issues every day, but I feel like I have a great support system of friends and family. I try to be as open as I can about my TS. When I'm dating a girl, I usually bring up the subject on the first or second date. Once I was on a date with a girl, she asked why I was blinking so much. I told her that my contacts were dry. She said, "Oh. I thought you had Tourette or something." I said, "No." She said, "Because my former roommate's boyfriend had Tourette's and it was so annoying. We would be watching TV and every few seconds I'd hear a high pitch, funny noise." I thought about it for a second and told her I had TS. I was open about it and explained the disorder and what exacerbates it. She said, "I feel like an asshole." I was understanding. She didn't know, and I'm sure it is annoying to hear an odd noise every few seconds when you're trying to relax, but I was happy to dispel some other negative thoughts she may have had.

There are so many negative and false views about Tourette syndrome, and the truth is, we are high-functioning individuals. It can be exhausting from the medications and the ticcing, along with lots of physical and mental pain, but we overcome it and face it. I try very hard. I give 125% to equal someone else's 85%.

Juliet 5

"I married the man that saved my life"

I am the lovely Juliet. Now it's not nice to ask a lady her age, but if you must know, I'm twenty-six years young. Originally, I'm from Chicago, but now I live in eastern Pennsylvania, right between the Crayola factory and the Peeps factory. I'm also right down the road from Pennsylvania's famous Hershey Park; I guess you can say in a kid's paradise. It's pretty cool. The paradise I don't live in is that I have Tourette syndrome, and all of those pesky underlying disorders that come with it, OCD, ADHD, and anxiety disorder. You know, pretty much all the classic symptoms of TS. I was officially diagnosed when I was twenty, but I thought I had my answer when I was thirteen thanks to the Internet. I wish I would have been able to say something about it then but I just didn't think I could.

I first started having tics when I was around ten or eleven, right after we moved from Illinois to New Jersey. It started with this weird thing in my right arm and some facial grimacing, which I still have. It was scary, I didn't know what was wrong. I went from my happy, normal life out in the burbs, to living in the woods in New Jersey with no one I knew. My father was gone all the time, and I thought my life was falling apart. I thought I was going to die and that's how it was and I should get used to it. Somewhat morbid, but that's how my mind was working.

Around that same time, I started another tic where I would lick my top and bottom lip until they were raw. I did this to the point they were brown and scared. It was awful. My mother didn't understand why I would do this to myself, but I couldn't help it. At first it felt like I had to do it, but then it was hurting so I had to lick it again. It was a constant cycle of my tic, and my OCD. I needed to make it stop hurting, so the only way to do that was to lick it again. My mother just didn't understand. She just didn't get it, was I doing this to hurt myself or just to do it. Then one day it just went away. I still have the tic, or the urge, but I try to restrain myself.

I didn't know what was going on and the worst part of it was that I wasn't even sure how to talk about it. My mom would always go on about how her perfect her pregnancy was, so nothing should be wrong with me. I felt like if I said anything to them I would be a failure. I just thought it was something terrible like a brain tumor. I also thought I could make them go way. That was clearly not true, what a joke. I still feel that way sometimes, like if I just try a little harder it'll go away and I'll be normal again, as I was before we moved. I didn't know better, but sometimes it's a nice dream.

There wasn't much said from my friends and parents. My parents were overwhelmed by my TS. They didn't know if I had ants in my pants, or what. Was I just that kind of kid or was there something wrong with me? I always had to move, I just couldn't stand still. I think my friends just looked right through my tics. We were all part of that outcast group; band geeks, choir nerds. I've been lucky; most people who I call friends haven't been rude enough to get in my face about it.

School was hell; nobody got it. It just seemed like nobody noticed that I had this full body jerking motion. There was nothing for kids with TS, or even kids with any type of disabilities. There was just nothing that accommodated anyone with special needs. My TS was ignored for the most part. If anyone had half a brain in any of those schools they would have seen it and said something more useful to my parents and maybe got me some help sooner.

For my whole life my tics have gotten worse around thanks-giving, I don't know why, but that's my TS. It would last through Christmas and eventually calm down in January. My parents would threaten to take me to a new doctor and I knew I could say that they would get better after the holidays, once the holiday stress was gone. My father would threaten to call the mental hospital and ship me off. One night when I was about twelve years old, my parents thought they would show me what I looked like when I was having my grimacing tic and shoulder-jerking tic. They made me stand next to them in the mirror so I could see what I looked like. My mother was the one who stood there to show me. She made all these awful motions with her face and was contorting her body. I just wanted to disappear. I wanted to run away, vanish, and never come back. I still want to cry when I think about it. I knew what I looked like. I knew how I felt. I knew that it was bad, but we went to doctors and no one said anything. I thought I knew what I had because of the Internet, but I wasn't going to say anything to my mother. I didn't have the language, or the understanding, to do so, but they showed me. I never really forgave them for that. They don't remember doing that to me, it wasn't that big of a deal to them, but I remember. I wish I could forget.

I feel like most of my family doesn't give a rat's backside about my TS, except my mom. My mom accepts me; she just doesn't, or can't, accept my TS. She always gets weird about it. It's as if she thinks it's a personal attack on her. She doesn't understand why I have this and always makes me feel like it's about her. All about her "perfect pregnancy" and I should have nothing wrong with me. My father doesn't get it either, but he's never been a big one with words. He doesn't talk too much. He just thinks the drug companies are out to make money off him and I'm just fine. I'm not really in touch with most of my family, so no one really knows the extent of my TS. As for my friends, I have not changed them a lot. The most important ones know about my TS, and they understand. They were there when I got my official diagnosis, and we celebrated that we had an answer. Now we just don't talk about it and I like it better that way.

My tics started with only motor tics, and then the vocal started. Those were the most embarrassing. I had throat clearing, nose snuffing, and other sounds that no one understood. When I first started ticcing, I had no control at all over it. I think the biggest change is that I've gotten older and the tics have gotten worse. I've been able to hide them more and make myself appear more and more normal. It has not always been easy to suppress them, but it was something that I had to learn how to do, or have my parents threaten to ship me off to the nut house. They always thought I was just doing this for attention. It's been a hard thing to deal with, but once I was able to get it a little more under control, I think the whole TS thing started to improve.

When I was twenty, I was big into playing online video games. It was my escape. I met a guy online playing one of those games. That guy would end up being my future husband, and save my life. Over the next year, we got to know each other online, but never met. One day we got on video chat, and at this point in my life, my tics were pretty bad. I still had no official diagnosis and doctors had me on a cocktail of medications. I was taking about sixteen different medications. I was scrawny, sickly thin, and pretty much bald from all the drugs I was on. He noticed my tics and knew something was wrong with me. He got in his car and drove thirteen hours from Maine to sit with me at the doctors. We went to the doctor who noticed my tics and asked me a bunch of questions, telling me afterward that I had seizures. I was crying my eyes out as he told me I had to go to a neurologist right away. I called my mother hysterical.

We went to the neurologist, and the doctor's assistant told me it looked as if I had a dystonic reaction, due to all the drugs I was on. I had no idea what that was, but I was giving Mirapex and I thought it was working, but I had to go for all these tests anyways. They did all the tests—MRI, CAT, blood work—and I had the "up all night" EEG. When we went back for the results, the doctor said I was fine, he found nothing wrong. Once again, I balled my eyes out. The doctor said I needed to find good psychiatric help because I appeared to have serious mental illness and needed help.

My future husband recommended I find a new doctor and get a second opinion. A few months later, and a redo of all the tests, the doctor looked at me and told me without any question I was a text book article for Tourette syndrome. He had no doubt of it. He even called a bunch of medical students in to look me over and check me out too. I felt so relieved at this point. "I'm not insane," I thought. It all started making sense. My future husband stuck by me with all of these doctors appointment. I ended up marrying that man who saved my life, and within two years, my hair did grow back.

It was a huge struggle to get over the idea that I wasn't insane. As weird as it sounds, I was always told that I was a mental patient and should be locked away. I never really had to come to terms with it until I had started seeing a psychologist and started discussing all of the labels attached to me at one time. I was forced to confront the part of me that assumed I was still insane. There wasn't any crazy here! I had to deal with it and accept who I am.

Since then I have had good days and bad days. Sometimes I feel like it's okay. I don't know anything different anymore, so why fight it. I have my answer, so that's good. Other days I worry about my future. I worry about my kids I want to have. I worry about what will happen if my tics don't get better; so far, all of the research says that they do, but I have yet to experience it. They are the same day to day, so I just try to adapt to it the best way I can.

I had many dreams in my life, especially dream jobs. So far, everything I wanted to be I realized I'm not going to get to be. It's really frustrating. I wanted to be an opera singer, but let my TS get in the way. I thought I'd be a music teacher, but I let my TS and a couple people get in the way of that too. Then I thought about perusing a career in physical therapy, but my mom told me I did not have the temperament for it, so I quit that too. I did go to school and got my masters in Theology, hoping I could teach Islamic studies and new religious movements, but I need a PhD to do that. It will take me a little bit to get there. I'd also love to be a bakery manager. I want to teach people how to decorate cakes for one of the giant bakery supply companies.

I currently do work at a bakery and love it. Some of the people I've worked with have made fun of me and some of them were okay with my TS. It took me a long time to tell people that I had TS. The people who I have the most important relationships with always treated me nice. The ones that were mean made me feel bad, and I spent a lot of time being sad. In the end, the ignorant people go away, and the important people stick around. There are always going to be the ones who make jokes about it, but it just doesn't even seem worth it to report them anymore. I just let it go and go home and complain to my husband. Now I have a great husband who puts up with all my bitching and my stuff. I just try to keep people from seeing my tics when they are at their worse because it makes me upset to talk about it.

My TS affects every part of my daily life because I just can't get away from it. Most days I can get up, brush my teeth, and watch some TV before my tics start. I really enjoy those few minutes of normalcy. The sad thing is I don't usually think about it until I'm about to punch into work and I realize that the rest of the tics and OCD are back to their normal level. It keeps me going for a bit during the day to know I'll have something to look forward to again in the morning. It makes me happy. The annoying part is that they pick up more when I start falling asleep. I feel as if it's a constant part of my life. I bump into stuff with my motor tic in my right arm. I crack my neck and irritate myself with other tics. And if it's not the tics, it's the OCD and anxiety that go with it. On a good day, I don't think about it too much, but on a bad day, I just want to cry. God, I wish it would go away. With my OCDs, I have symmetry issues, cleaning issues, and body issues. I need things in a straight line, and at work, things need to be in ROT G BIV order for coloring, sprinkles, and icing. It makes everyone at work nuts, but me.

One of my biggest tic and OCDs has to do with my teeth. My teeth are very dull from my chattering tic, which then triggers my OCD. I always think there is something wrong with my teeth. If I get a cavity, I have to check it with a mirror a million times and stress myself out about it. I just worry about all this little crap to the point that I just cry. I will keep on looking at my teeth to see if they are getting better or worse. Then I worry that the dentist is going to yell at me when I go for being a "bad girl" and not being able to hold still.

At the end of the day, I just try to relax. I like to play games on my computer where I don't have to think about stuff. I can leave my TS behind me. I love to get home and just hang out and talk to my husband and have a nice evening. I have fish, and taking care of them helps take some of the edge off. I also make jewelry and love doing gigantic puzzles.

My parents tried; they did what they could with what they knew at the time. Would I like to think that more could have been done? Yes. I'm still mad at them about some stuff, but when I was growing up, things were a lot different. My dad was away most of the time working, and it was just my mom and me. She was awesome. She tried so hard and lord knows I was a difficult kid to deal with. I was such a handful for her with all the stuff that just went wrong all at one time.

We all have something. I have TS, but I still achieve what I have to. I am a professional cake decorator. I do stacked and tiered wedding cakes, drawing, and you name it. I'm actually one of the best decorators in the company that I work for. Yeah, really! So next time someone tells you that you can't do something because you have Tourette syndrome, or any other type of disability, remember me. I have a bad movement disorder and every day I make beautiful wedding and birthday cakes, delicate, decorative things that I should not be able to do, but I do. I hope to have my own bakery by the end of 2012.

I want to end this with: I have Tourette syndrome; it's part of my life. I can never and will never escape it. There's no way out, or even a treatment that works for each person. TS is a part of me that drives me insane every day; it's a part of me that I never wanted. I don't want to deal with it, and if I could, I would get rid of it in a heartbeat, but I cannot escape from it or its co-morbid conditions. I have to learn to live with them, learn to live with who I am and just deal with it because it is who I am. What I'd want people to know about my TS and me is simple. I'm just Juliet, I have Tourette syndrome and it has me, and I'm just fine. We have answers and have something to say.

Matthew 6

"Just happy it has a name!"

My name is Matthew. I am twenty-six from Danville, Illinois. Mine is a strange story. I was only diagnosed a year ago at the age of twenty-five. Even after thirteen years of searching for a diagnosis, and almost twenty years of suffering from tics. I started experiencing tics at around six or seven years old. It was a really hard time and thing for me to go through. When I first started ticcing, it was horrible; I felt like a freak. I didn't know what was going on, what I was doing, or when it would stop. Even without the ticcing, I would succumb to teasing—I was always the fat kid.

My close friends were great, and they were really cool about my ticcing. They would often ask me what I was doing, and since I had no idea that they were considered tics, I would just blame it on a sore neck, and/or shoulders. I had an excuse for everything I did, but they accepted me, even with all my odd behaviors and things I did. I can't say the same for all my classmates. The same fact of not knowing what was causing theses tics did not provide for an easy time in school. I never talked about it in school because I didn't know what it was. If I were ticcing in school, kids would always ask me, "What are you doing?" Or, "Why are you doing that?" I would usually quickly change the subject. I was constantly picked on and teased by my classmates. They would make fun of my head jerking, and vocal tics. Kids would get in my face and jerk their heads around, mimicking my tics, and call me "bobblehead." As a result, I spent a lot of the time hiding and holding in my tics as much as I possibly could.

There always seemed to be some type of difficulty in school. I never had any special accommodations, but I do remember having issues. One thing was reading. It always came a little difficult to keep my place while reading due to my head jerking. I also remember having a specific issue with my third grade teacher. This is around the time where I was having many vocal tics, and she did not like this. In fact, I don't think she liked me altogether. The disruption of her class often aggravated her and she would come over to my desk, flip it over, tossing everything to the floor, and leaving me to clean it up. I suffered such embarrassment and anxiety due to my tics, but this event would only mortify me even more. It was almost written approval for my classmates to continue to taunt me. "Hey, if the teacher can, why can't we?" Because of these vocal tics, my nickname throughout my childhood was "Blurt." I was a very loud child with many vocal sounds. I made animal sounds, screams, chirps, and so on. My family just thought I was a silly kid, and in reality, I was a crazy wild kid, so my mother just figured what I was doing was part of my personality. Every night would usually end the same. I would go to bed and tic away in the comfort and privacy of my room, and my mother would yell at me through the wall, "Shut up and go to bed, Matt!"

When the more physical tics began, my mother's concern set in. When we spoke to my pediatrician, he nonchalantly said they were normal things that boys do and that they would go away. Well, obviously they didn't. When I was about ten or fourteen, we started looking for some sort of answer. By this point, the head jerking and shoulder shrugging started causing horrific pains and headaches. We were not so well to do, actually, we were kind of on the poor side. We did not have insurance, but we kids did have state-issued medical cards. With the medical cards, we were only able to see doctors on a preferred list. All of these ended up being duds. The doctor was more concerned with the pain being caused by the tics, rather than the tics themselves or their cause. He told my mother I was doing the tics to compensate for the pain in my neck and he wanted to do an MRI, a CT scan, and some X-rays. All of the tests came back with no abnormalities, so we were pretty much given the brush off.

We made another attempt when I was about fifteen or sixteen, but this time we tried the chiropractic route, due to the headaches, muscular tightening, and joint grinding. Once again, he ordered an MRI, a CT scan, and X-rays. Once again, all was normal. I was just told that the reason the tics were happening were due to the extreme tightness in my neck. They could not explain why I was so tight, so I just kept ticcing away.

When I was about seventeen and a half, I figured the third time was a charm, plus I knew my medical card would end when I was eighteen, so this might be my last chance for a while. I was filled with frustration and I needed answers; I needed to find out why these things were happening to my body and why they wouldn't stop. This time was a little different, seeing I was referred to a specialist. I figured this was a good sign; he was bound to figure out something, being in the top of his field of work. As usual, we did the same tests as I had done numerous times before. He called us in to discuss the results and said everything was normal. We brought up the history of my tics, and at this point, he laughed at me, told me to "stop it," and then began to mimic my tics in front of me. I was absolutely crushed. We had been searching for an answer for almost eight years to find nothing, and to top it off, I was almost 18 and wouldn't be able to use the medical card.

I tried to take the doctor's advice and "stop it." I worked hard to try to hide my tics, suppress them. I actually became really good at it, but I also became very depressed. Hiding my tics was hiding who I was. I didn't have many friends, and if I weren't in school, I would just hide in my room. It was my safe place. I couldn't suppress all of my tics all of the time, so once I was in my room, I could release them all. I was afraid if I did them out in public, I would scare people, or they wouldn't understand me even though I couldn't help it. I was just very confused and uninformed. I thought what I was doing might have been bad behavior that became a bad habit. A habit I couldn't break. No matter how hard I tried to stop, the worse they would get.

I've had so many tics it's hard to keep track. Some were different when I was young, but I also have a lot of the same ones. When I was younger, I had the head turning, shoulder shrugging, hand and finger tics. For many years I would take my hands and wrap them up in my shirt and stretch it out. I went through a lot of shirts due to creating holes in them. Now my tics are neck jerking, head shaking, shoulder shrugging, lip licking, face grimacing, toe tapping, sniffing, some minor sounds, and on occasion, repeating words. I have many of the same tics as I did when I first started, but over the years, they have just become more elaborate, except vocally. I'm less vocal now than when I was younger, now I just have a low-pitch grunt and a high-pitch sniff.

When I was twenty, I started working as a nursing assistant, and I love it. I get to help people and truly make a difference in their lives and it felt good. I would hold in the tics I could, and the ones that did come out I would just blame on a stiff neck, allergies, or muscle spasms. Basically, even as an adult, every tic had an excuse, and my coworkers accepted them. I continued working in nursing and was hired on at a veteran's hospital. My dream had come true; I'm an employee of the federal government! With the new job, came benefits. I could finally go to the doctor.

I decided to go to the doctor, but just to try to get something for the joint and muscle pain. Due to the years of neck and shoulder tics, I just have such pain. I wasn't even worried about the tics anymore, I just figured I'd keep hiding them as well as I could and just get something for the pain. I was referred to an orthopedic doctor in the area. He did some tests and we tried several medications and joint injections with no result. After a few appointments, I did come clean about a few of my tics. He said he noticed, but just thought it was a nervous thing I did. He then referred me to another pain specialist. While in the examination room waiting to see this new doctor, something told me, "Don't hide your tics." When the doctor came in, I just let them out as if I was in my room at home, my safe spot. He did his exam and listened to my history of doctors, tests, and problems. He told me that from what he had observed, I had the classic symptoms of Tourette syndrome and for me to go to a neurologist for a thorough look over.

I left the office and drove home. When I got home, I went straight to my room and just broke down crying. I was so happy it had a name. I started doing a lot of research on the syndrome. It was amazing; everything I read about it was like reading my story on paper. All of these tics, these feelings, other people have experienced too. At twenty-five years old, I finally felt like a whole person.

I did some research on neurologists in the area and found one about forty-five minutes away from me who specializes with movement disorders. I made an appointment. He agreed it was Tourette syndrome, and gave me a DX (diagnosis) of ADHD, OCD, and general anxiety disorder. He then sent me to Chicago to the Northwestern Movement Clinic where I was seen by the head of TS Education for Northwestern University School of Neurology. She was the third confirmation for TS.

It was a very long and stressful diagnosis process and I'm glad it was finally over. Having a diagnosis has not improved my tics in any way, but there's a difference in ticcing and not knowing why, and ticcing and being able to explain why. I often felt like I was living a double life when I was undiagnosed. Now I can be me and stop hiding. I could be open with friends and coworkers. When I went to work and told my coworkers my diagnosis, they were not that shocked. Some of them actually said, "Oh, that explains it." I guess I didn't hide my tics as well as I thought I did. I noticed now that I get treated the same, but that I get watched a lot more. It's as if they are just watching and waiting for me to tic, so I often feel like I'm on display.

I have a lot of worries with work. I guess this is part of the anxiety disorder, or the OCD. I worry that my patients are going to think less of me and think that I will not be able to give them the best care. I'm always worried about being fired for my TS, and scared my coworkers won't take me seriously. We live in a world of judgment and I constantly feel I am being judged. I'm trying to be more open about my TS. I even typed up a paper about my TS and myself and passed it out to all my coworkers. This was and is all so new to me and not sure how to be proactive about it, but it's a good first step.

For me, having TS is a daily struggle. I don't like looking at myself in the mirror, especially when I'm ticcing; I hate the way I look. I start ticcing between thirty to forty-five minutes after I wake up and don't stop until I go to sleep. When I start to wake up, my mind starts going in overdrive, the obsessive thoughts start. I obsess about what happened yesterday, and what's going to happen today. When it's warm out, I do like to spin my flag; I was in color guard when I was in high school, and now I am a choreographer. It is one thing I can do and not tic. It's kind of my outlet.

Right now, I'm on Tenex for my tics and its working great. I still have tics but they have gone down greatly. I'm also on Xanax for the anxiety and OCD, which helps to just take the edge off. I still deal with my OCDs and anxiety. Going out with other people, I'm usually worried about trying to hide my tics. I usually end up shutting down and not my usual fun self. Depending on where I am, I always sit in the back of the room. I don't like people behind me, sitting or walking. I always watch what people are doing, and like the comfort of ticcing without anyone noticing. If someone is behind me, I feel like I'm on display, all I can think is, "Are they watching me?" I just have a lot of anxiety with people. I don't like being touched either. I know my mother is hurt by this, but I don't even like having her touch me, I can't help it. This is why I spend so much time in my safe spot, my bedroom.

As for my OCD, where do I start? Sometimes it controls my life. My compulsions revolve around straightening, checking, cleaning, and especially counting. I count everything in a room and then see if it is divisible by three. If it is not, I have to mentally work it until it fits my little equation. My life revolves around the number three. I do things in three; I lock my car in threes, I walk in threes, I lock doors in threes, and check them in threes. As I leave a room, I count my steps; they have to be divisible by three before I can leave the room. I even wash my hands in threes, and since I have two hands, that's six squirts of soap and six paper towels. It has nothing to do with germs, I just have so many racing thoughts going on in my head that I try to fill my head with meaningless numbers to overpower the thoughts. If there is nothing to count, I figure out something to count so I can calm my OCD thoughts down.

Some of my obsessive thoughts are, "I'm going to get fired," "I'm going to die alone," "No one loves me," and "People are going to kill my family." If anyone is late, I will start obsessing that they are dead. I also have what I call "the bad thoughts," while watching TV or talking with someone, I suddenly have thoughts of hurting them. I hate these thoughts because I am a very nice and caring person and would never do any of these things. It's just scary sometimes in my head.

I tic a lot in the evening, mainly because I try to suppress the tics I can during the day and then they all come out when I get home. I have my nightly rituals to help me calm down and get to sleep. I have to clean and bleach the kitchen, I'm not sure why but I find the smell of bleach calming. I have to make sure everything is in its place, and clean and organized. I try to straighten the rest of the house too without waking my family. So basically, I am sneaking around the house at night cleaning. Once I am finished, I lock the doors. This is a whole process in itself. Three locks per door and checking each door handle by giggling nine times three so I shake each one twenty-seven times so I know they are locked and my family is safe. Then it is off to my room where I begin to straighten my closet and dresser and put my shoes back to where they belong.

The day I finally received my diagnosis was the happiest day of my life. We had been searching for an answer for almost sixteen years, and I finally had a name for it. It meant the world to me. I didn't have to lie anymore, and if people asked why I did the things I did, I could tell them. It's a curse in a sense, I'm always in pain and anxious, but in a way it has made who I am today. I am a compassionate, loving, goofy, fun person. I don't think I would be the same person without these qualities. We are all different and have our own personal set of challenges and problems, mine are just more obvious. Now that I have a diagnosis, I can just be myself. It will take me time to gain confidence to be more open about my TS, but when it comes down to it, "It has a name!"

Meredith 7

"Wish I was more open about my TS; I'd shout it from the rooftops"

My name is Meredith and I have Tourette syndrome. Wow, that's really weird to say, I usually never say that. I'm twenty-seven years old and live in Westchester, New York. I have spent my whole life in the so-called "TS closet." I try to keep it to myself. I'm trying to be more open about it and try to educate but it's hard. I am constantly thinking, "What if I tell them and they don't want to be my friend, or want nothing to do with me." It scares me.

I was diagnosed with Multiple Tic Disorder when I was seven, and then fully diagnosed with TS at the age eleven. After I received the diagnosis, I cried. I remember sitting on my mom's bed crying with her. I was crying because this thing that I was struggling with for so many years finally had a name, but also I knew I would have this condition for the rest of my life and that there was no cure. After the initial reaction, I think I just kept a lot of it to myself. I didn't like to talk about, not even with my family. It was frustrating at first because I knew I couldn't control the tics. It was like a burst of energy that just had to come out no matter what, and that particular tic was the energies only outlet. It's annoying when you feel you have to do something, but you don't know the reason behind why you have to do it.

The day after I received my diagnosis my mother called my school and discussed the situation with my teachers. I ended up staying home from school that day and the two sixth grade classes had a meeting about my TS and me. I have no idea what was said but imagine it had something to do with educating them about TS. Informing them not to treat me different, I could not help what I do. Later that day I went to the store with my mother and I saw a girl from my class. I asked her how the assembly went about me, she said it went well and that she had no idea I had TS. After the assembly, everything stayed the same, no one treated me any differently than they did before they knew. At this point I had very few friends, I'm not sure if this had anything to do with my TS or not. I guess I'll never know, but it has always been a thought in my mind.

Most of my adolescence was spent hiding my TS and not talking about it. All I wanted as a child was to have friends, and maybe a boyfriend. I just wanted to be normal and focus all my energy into achieving this. In my mind, having TS was not normal and I was ashamed by it, so I just didn't talk about it. I was afraid to tell anyone, but my mother wanted me to talk about it. I didn't have many friends around the time I was diagnosed, so my mother tried to get me to talk to my cousin who I was very close to. I didn't even want to talk to her for fear that she would judge me, or worse yet, not want to play with me anymore.

I guess "normal" was the key word for me in school. The school district was very accommodating to my TS and me. I had a 504 but I rarely ever used it. I very much wanted to be normal and using any kind of testing modification made me feel less normal. I was lucky, though; it was there if I did decide to use these modifications.

As for the underlying disorder, I was never diagnosed with any of the disorders usually associated with TS, but I definitely think I have some. I like to say I have OCD tendencies. I had this thing that if someone moves something, I have to move it back to its original spot. I still have this a little, but it was much more of an issue when I was younger. When I was younger, my friends would come over and we'd hang out in my room. They would move things around in my room just to see me move it back. I had to put it back in its place. Everything in my room had its place or right spot and it needed to remain there. For me the tics are the worst part of TS, not the underlying disorders. OCD is something I could hide, but I could not always hide my tics. When the tics are bad and in full force, watch out world.

For the most part my adolescence years weren't too bad. I spent most of the time trying to hide my tics and be normal. When I entered seventh grade and a new school, I made a few new friends, but still didn't tell them about the TS. It's hard when making new friends to burden them with something so personal to you. I suppose the only issue I did have was my classmates. A lot of them called me "tic girl." While I probably should have been offended by that, I actually just laughed it off. I thought of it more as a compliment, "Hey, they were paying so much attention to me that they gave me a nickname."

In high school, I developed a friendship with a girl. We became very close and planned a trip to Europe. On this trip, we were going to be traveling from city to city and sharing hotels along the way. I had not told her that I had TS and I started to stress out about it. I wasn't sure if I would be able to suppress my tic the whole time. By the time we got to Paris, the second city on our trip, I told her.

I had to tell her; otherwise, she was going to start noticing the tics, especially the vocal ones. I said, "I have this thing and I can't hold it in anymore. I'm going to start making noises soon." I was so nervous in telling her, but her response was totally not what I expected. She just said, "Whatever. Do what you have to do." I had built up in my mind how I thought she was going to react, and it was the polar opposite. I felt like she was going to judge me, but instead I was actually given the opportunity to educate her. I had a sort of feeling of acceptance. She then went on to ask me questions, "Does it hurt?" What's it feel like?" After that we never really spoke of it again, there was never a reason too.

I can't say this situation helped me open up more about my TS, as I was still quite insecure. My sophomore year in college I was dating this guy. We had been dating for a while and I felt like it was starting to get serious, but I didn't feel like we would be able to get any more serious unless I was honest about my TS. How could it progress if I wasn't truthful? One day we were sitting on my bed in my dorm room and I said, "I have to tell you something." I told him and he said, "Yeah, I know." I was shocked! "How did you know?" He told me he asked his mother why I blinked my eyes so much and she told him that I had TS. I asked him if it was going to be a problem, was he going to be able to deal with it. He said it was fine and that he didn't care. I guess he really didn't because he is now my fiancé. Even now, he tells me all the time that he doesn't even notice it anymore. "You don't have TS, you're just the pretty girl I'm in love with," he says. I have so many fears about being honest with people but I guess for the most part my fears are unwarranted.

Although the tics I embody are obvious, I still don't like to talk about my TS with people, or introduce people to it. My TS is essentially something that I deal with on my own. It still takes a lot for me to tell even my close friends. I am very picky and choosy about whom I tell. I still have a fear that they will want nothing to do with me, which is ridiculous. I think part of growing up with TS all my life has left me with emotional scarring. I worry that if I tell people, they won't want to be my friend or deal with me because of my TS. Even at twenty-seven years old, it's a struggle. When I do get the courage to tell someone, I pray and pray that they will still want to be associated with me now that they know the name behind my tics.

I don't know why I can't get over my fear of telling people. I know at this stage in my life I am accepted. No one asks me about my tics, except on a rare occasion. My fiancé will sometimes ask me if a noise I make is a tic. Sometimes it is; sometimes it's not. I can suppress my tics a lot more now so people don't notice them as much, but sometimes they will come out. There was one time in was on the phone with a friend and she asked me, "Are you okay, do you have the hiccups?" I told her, "No, that was a tic." She said, "Oh, okay." The conversation went on as normal.

I am slowly coming to terms with the fact I have TS and I need to discuss it more, but those conversation are still limited. I recently went out to dinner with a friend from middle school. She asked me if the whole thing with me moving things around to the right place was part of my TS, I told her yes.

Things like this get me thinking, what else is part of my TS. There are so many underlying disorders that can come out in so many different ways that I just don t know. There are many things that a can attribute to my TS and I always wonder if I didn't have TS would I still be afflicted with these conditions. I have to eat my food fast because if I don't the other person I'm eating with might eat it. I also have horrible hand coordination, which causes bad handwriting, and the inability to cut a straight line. If I'm at work and I have to cut things, I tell my boss or coworker that I can't cut very nicely and the end project will come out better if someone else does it. People are understanding and appreciative of my honesty, but it is truly embarrassing. I also have this thing where I have to touch my ring finger to the page as I'm writing because it feels right.

I also get anxiety, specifically when it comes to getting to places on time. I hate being late. If I'm waiting for another person to get ready, I get very anxious and my tics get harder and louder. I attribute that, whether fairly or not, to my TS. So while I was technically never diagnosed with some of those underlying conditions, I tend to think I do exhibit a few of them.

TS affects different aspects of my daily life. When I'm walking down the street, I wonder if people notice my tics and what they think. I'm always worried about what strangers who don't even know me or understand my tics think about me. When I walk past someone and I grunt, do they hear me even though I'm trying to suppress them? When I am blinking really badly and almost walk into a coworker, do they know I was ticcing or do they just think I was not paying attention to where I was walking? I worry about how long I will be able to suppress my tics until they have to come out full force. All of these thoughts run through my head multiple times a day. My tics and how others perceive them is something I struggle with all the time, every day. All I can do is try to suppress them as well as I can, but once I get home, all bets are off… I begin ticcing up a storm and let loose.

My tics are most present at night, I think that's because I do suppress them all day. When I get home at night, they all come out full force. I usually try to watch some TV, it relaxes me. It takes me away from the days problems, and drama, and lets me forget about everything I have to do the next day. It's one thing that doesn't trigger me. Sometimes I feel like everything is a trigger, caffeine, alcohol, hormonal changes, stress, and anxiety. You name it and I can probably point to it as a trigger for my tics. Having TS sucks! I drink alcohol, it sucks; I drink caffeine, it sucks. There are just too many triggers, but it's something I live with. I just try to live my life the best I can, and suppress what I can, when I can.

I like to have a drink socially occasionally, but it's hard. I know it makes my tics worse, especially wine. I have noticed that even the day after my tics are still bad. When my tics are bad, my fiancé will ask me what's causing the tics. He usually assumes I'm stressed with work or something, but I tell him, "No, it's from that wine we drank last night." I just want to be normal, and most people my age go out for drinks, but I know I'm going to pay for it later.

My tics have definitely waxed and waned a lot over the years. During puberty, it was horrible. I had very loud and obvious vocal tics. Even now, whenever I get my period, my tics get pretty bad, I guess do to the increase in hormones. I have been taking birth control that makes me get less periods in order to control the hormones. It helps a little bit, but I don't recall a time in my life when the tics were in control or nonexistent.

Throughout my diagnosis, I have tried quite a few medications. Doctors have put me on Tenex, Klonopin, Klonopin patches, and Prozac. I don't think any of the medications helped me at all; they just made me tired. I had no life, and I just wanted to sleep. At one point, we also tried a holistic approach. I was on dozens of vitamins, which didn't help either. Looking back, it was a crock of shit, a waste of my money. I know everyone is different and maybe these methods might work for someone else, but unfortunately, it didn't for me.

I am still coming to terms with my TS. At my age, I know what my tics are and how to cope with them, but if I were fully comfortably with my TS, I wouldn't have a problem telling ANYONE about my disorder. I kind of wish I was at that point, but I'm not. The Tourette Syndrome Association has helped me come out of my closet a little. It's been an invaluable recourse for me. I started getting involved right out of college. I started going to support groups, but felt that they were more geared to parents and their children. I was twenty-four years old and not interested in what children were going through in school, I've been there and it sucks. I was looking for something I could relate to as a young adult. Then I heard about a gala that the NYC chapter of the Tourette Syndrome Association was having. I went and made friends with some of the board members and found out about their "Friends of the TSA Social Hour." It's a monthly get together for adults with TS and their friends were we all just hang out at a lounge. I felt like I could relate to all the people and compare stories.

I wish I had the courage to tell people about my TS, I think I would shout it from the rooftops, "IM A TOURETTER!" Really, I would, but I don't want to talk about my tics too much. I think there's a fine line between educating people and about TS and boring them with the everyday nuisances of it. While TS is part of my life, I let it be a small part; I don't like to dwell on it. Nonetheless, as cliché as it sounds, I don't think I would be who I am today had it not been my struggle with TS. I like to think it made me a stronger person. I think I have matured enough and realized that having TS and dealing with my tics is part of who I am, it's shaped the woman I am today.

I feel blessed, in a way, that God decided to give me TS and not some horrible disease. TS is manageable for me, as much as it sucks when my tics are out of control. I truly believe that God would not give me something I could not handle. Therefore, I take it as a compliment that God thinks I'm strong enough to handle TS, because let me tell you, dealing with it on a day-to-day basis can be quite a challenge, and I struggle through it.

I desperately hope they find a cure, and fast. Not just for me, but also for the countless others, the newly diagnosed, the closeted TSers, or the ones who don't even know they have it. I feel for those people. I know what it's like to be constantly hiding something, or making up excuse after excuse for why I'm doing what I'm doing. The most important ones are the children. The ones struggling through the stares from the other kids, I just want to educate their little minds in a way that they will comprehend. I just want people to know that I'm a normal person, despite my obvious tics, and so are all the other TSers.

Chelsea 8

"Watch me own it!"

I'm Chelsea, just a twenty-nine-year-old girl, no I'm a woman! Hear me roar, RAH! Oops, sorry, I don't know why I'm screaming already, we just started this. Maybe I have Tourette syndrome. By the way, I'm a comedian living in NYC. Just to let you know, I do have TS, but I don't have coprolalia. So if I call you an ass face or ass hat, I like that better, you more than likely deserved it. I'm also a freelance TV and video producer.

Originally, I'm from Clarion, PA. I was diagnosed at four years old. The first tics I remember was feeling that I had to squeeze my eyes shut, squeeze my fingers into a fist, and curl my toes as hard as I could. I remember my parents asking me why I felt the need and I couldn't explain. I just didn't feel right if I didn't do it. It took them about a year to diagnose me, originally I was diagnosed with epilepsy, but being four, I don't remember much. I feel fortunate to be diagnosed at such a young age, so as long as I can remember I understood why I was ticcing. Since I was so young, there was no dealing process. It was always just a part of who I was.

My family was great. I owe them a lot, maybe a big mansion if I hit it big. My mother has a degree in Early Education, and she knew it was TS as soon as I started exhibiting tics at two or three and started taking me to different doctors. We got the diagnosis, and she always kept the conversation going, and made me feel it was under control. She said everyone has their thing, and I should let them know if I wanted to take medications. I never did.

I was also fortunate to have a great relationship with my teachers and administrators because of my parents. It made it a little easier having a mother who was an educator and a father who was an administrator, who later became the principle and superintendent of my high school. They knew the right channels to go through to make sure my school had the right information, so I had a little advantage in that regard. There weren't many school issues, but my TS was never so disruptive that I couldn't complete my work properly. I was always good in school, but I just had trouble absorbing the info. I'd take notes and have no idea what just happened. I'd look at my friend's notes and I asked, "When did that happen?" I thought I was paying attention, but I think I was concentrating on my tics. It definitely did take me longer to finish certain things and I was terrible at timed tests.

Despite the support and understanding from my family, I wasn't very open about my TS with my classmates. I was sometimes teased and questioned about my tics. I had a lot of eye related tics, and as I got older, my vocal tics increased and became more noticeable. I was constantly asked, "Why are you doing that?" or "Stop doing that!" I also go a lot of, "Do you know you're doing this?" (insert mimicking of tic) and "This is what you look like, Chelsea!" (insert mimic). I would just chalk it up to allergies or something in my eye. I'm sure many people knew me as the twitchy, weird girl, but it never progressed beyond that. I was able to control many of my more severe tics and hold them in until I got home. God bless my poor family.

I'm not sure what initially gave me the courage to be open and honest about my TS, I think I just reached a point where I realized it was more detrimental to keep it to myself. It wasn't until I was a senior in high school that I started feeling compelled to be more open about it. I had a lot of anxiety about telling people, saying the words out loud was a big deal and made me very uncomfortable at the time. I started thinking, "How can I educate and dispel all of the stereotypes of TS if I'm not even being honest with myself and those closest to me?" Since then it has become much easier, even second nature.

My friends were incredibly supportive. Every time I told someone, they would say something to the effect of, "Well, I guess I noticed you doing little things. I just figured that was just part of who you were." I couldn't think of a better or more supportive answer for them to give. It felt good to put something that was already obviously out there in the open for discussion instead of having it be the twitching elephant in the room. I think it made my friends feel better as well to know it was something that I was aware of, and they shouldn't feel uncomfortable when I'm ticcing, or wonder what I'm doing, or if I realized I was doing it.

After college and I moved to NYC, I felt it was finally time, and finally had the opportunity, to start advocating for others with TS and myself. I started volunteering with the NYC chapter of the TSA. Soon after volunteering, I was elected onto the board, then onto being the secretary of the board. I'm very excited to say that in 2012, I was elected as the chairperson for the board. I could not think of a better way to spread the word.

I think the best way I can describe a tic is the most intense itch you've ever had, but the itch is in your brain. The only way to scratch the itch is to do whatever movement or sound the brain is telling you to do. With life stresses and changes, there is a lot of waxing and waning with the tic. I could go months without experiencing a specific tic and wake up one morning and there it is again. My TS really spiked when I started college, and again when I moved to the city, but I find ways to deal with it. Really by now its second nature to me. I find ways to make my tics look like normal movements. I may wait until I have a reason to be shrugging my shoulders, or laugh to release a shoulder tic.

Funny story, sometimes I pretend to look behind me to release my neck tic, I just have the need to stretch the neck muscles. One time I was in a bodega picking up some groceries. I was walking down the aisle and felt that tic itch and I did my "look behind me tic." There was a woman behind me who noticed this. She continued shopping and went to the next isle. When I got to the next isle, she was still there, once again, I had to tic, and once again, she saw me. This tic is basically me just looking back over my shoulder, and I'm pretty sure she thought I was checking her out or eyeing her.

When I think about all the tics I have, I'm not sure how I have time to do anything else. It's time consuming, and sometimes painful. I wiggle my ears, which sounds harmless, but it gives me a headache and keeps me up at night. I nod my head so violently I swear I can feel my brain ricocheting in my skull. I also have a shoulder shrug tic, finger and wrist flicking tic, sniffing tic, and a crossing and rolling of the eyes tic. I don't do as many vocal tics now, but I used to have a high-pitched scream so high that I'd hurt my throat. There have also been times where I have pulled on the back of my head to feel that stretch and ended up screwing up my neck for days.

The scariest moment was when I had a tic that I had to bend over to feel a stretch in my back. I haven't done this one in a while, but one time I did it so violently I thought I paralyzed myself. There was such an intense pain from the bottom of my back to the top of my head. It was so painful I couldn't see. I thought, "Great, Chelsea, you're the first person in the world who has voluntarily paralyzed yourself." The rest of the day, I was convinced I moved one of my vertebrae, and by the end of the day, I was going to be paralyzed. I had a cool boss, who saw that there was something wrong and told me to go to the doctor. I walked into the doctor's office, looked her straight in the eye, and told her, "I'm here because I think I might be paralyzed later on." Wow, can you tell I have OCD too?

OCD is my jam! My OCD actually used to be worse than my tics. It used to take me hours to get ready for bed at night because I was trying to complete all of my rituals. I'm a bit of a neat freak, but I never really dealt with the type of OCD that revolves around cleaning or sterilizing. My OCDs would revolve around something bad happening to someone I loved. If I touched something or took a step and felt as though I was thinking of hell or had something red in my field of vision, I would have to redo or retouch the object. When I would re-step or touch, I would have to think, or even say aloud, "Heaven is good," or "Nothing bad," which is ironic because I'm not a religious person.

I also had a thing with the number three. I had to touch things in three, and do things in three. I don't remember how or why, or what I thought was going to happen, but I had to do it in three. Sixs and nines were also good, but I guess they are just multiples of threes so that made it okay.

For a while my tics where on an even keel, but it's a little worse lately, although still manageable. They really just wax and wane. I do have to say they are better than when I was younger, just worse than a few years ago. That's the way of TS. You can have a mild year, and then they just flare up. I think right now my tics are worse than my OCD, which is the complete opposite from when I was a kid. The rollercoaster of TS can be exhausting. I still find it annoying to have people ask me why I'm doing something, or when I notice people on the subway watching me, wondering why I'm making noises or movements, but most of the time I can shut that out.

I think for me one of the biggest things I do to help is exercise. I love to run. Some people say the ticcing stops when they exercise or engage in some type of activities, but I still tic when I run. It's always fun to go for a run and have people stare as I jog by. It could be that I'm just being self-conscious. I have been running since college, every morning, probably more than I should. This is just my time to disconnect from the rest of the world and get my thoughts together. I usually do about thirty minutes to an hour, depending on the day. A few years ago, I ran the NYC marathon for TEAM TSA, and it was the most incredible experience. I was delighted to do this for a cause that is so important to me.

I think at this point in my life I really just try to do what I can to somewhat control my tics. As the day goes on, they get worse, but not all the time. It's probably associated with what's going on in the day, and how I'm feeling rather than the time of day, but by the end of the day, they are generally worse. I know when I sleep more I tic less, so I try to make sure to get a good night sleep. The wiggling ears don't always help with that. That tic does have a history of keeping me up. Anxiety and stress are also a big tic trigger, and I'm sure certain foods have something to do with the tics, but I have yet to find any correlation.

At the end of the day, I just try to relax; maybe write or veg out watching some TV. A glass of wine always helps at the end of the day. I love my wine. I don't think I necessarily tic less when I drink, which I have heard others say it does with their tics, but it defiantly makes them less annoying. I guess it just makes it easier to deal with. I'm just not as annoyed with them when I have a glass of chardonnay with me.

I have found difficulty in telling stories if I'm excited or very emotional about the topic. One time I was trying to tell my roommate a story, and I was so excited I couldn't get the words out. My tics start to get in the way, and then my thoughts go out of control. I end up getting so scattered just trying to say what I want to say that I almost start stuttering. My brain just goes a million miles a minute trying to think of the story and the fact that my tics are going nuts. There's no down time for my mouth or brain, and it drives me crazy. It's hard to concentrate.

Besides being a comedian, I'm also a producer. I'm currently working at a live show and the only way to communicate with the other producers and staff is on headset. For example, if I want to talk to Charlie, I would say, "Chelsea for Charlie. Chelsea for Charlie," and wait for the response, "Go for Charlie." One day in the middle of the show, all I heard was some girl on the headset saying, "Oh my God, I know! It's like I have Tourette syndrome, I'm just swearing up a storm." It took everything inside me not to go, "CHELSEA TO EVERYONE!" Well, you could imagine what would come next, but I remained professional. I mean we were in the middle of a live show, and I was new to this job.

Don't get me wrong, I'm a big advocate on speaking out and being very open about my TS, but there's a place and time. I've actually recently started speaking at schools about TS and educating people about it. I start by showing a video of my comedy act to trick them into thinking I'm cool. Then I tell them I have TS. I ask them what they think when they hear "Tourette syndrome." They sometimes say swearing, and sometimes they are too nervous to say anything. I explain that TS is a neurological disorder, and it's not contagious. I inform them that we each have our things that make us different, whether it's the color of our hair, or that you have asthma, and dispel the stereotype that it's the, "swearing disorder." I demonstrate my tics for them then I bring two kids up to the chalkboard for a demonstration. I tell both kids to write their names ten times, as fast as they can, but one has to do one of my tics every time I say a body part. Of course the kid not ticcing finishes first, and I explain that this is what it's like most of the time for someone with TS. The kids start to open up after this, and tell me what makes them different. It's a great feeling to see them open up.

I have also done a few comedy shows called "Call us Crazy" with a friend of mine. It's a group of comedians with diagnosed disorders that joke, but making light of their disorder or differences. It's not just about TS. I have people with bipolar, OCD, eating disorder, depression, etc. It's been a big hit so far, and has educated a few more people about my disorder and other disorders.

It helped me to not talk about it when I was younger. I was ashamed and just didn't want to have the conversation. It's a hard thing to talk about, but once you start, it can be very therapeutic and you can keep spreading awareness. Now I think TS affects me in a positive way, I'm constantly reminded that everyone is dealing with something. I can't say I don't still get annoyed with people, but having TS conditions me to think twice about passing judgment. Now I just own it! You don't know me nor do I know you. You all think I'm weird, so I'm going to be weird. Watch me, I will own it.

I feel so fortunate to have TS because it has shaped me to who I am. It's really such a part of me and my self-concept that I can't imagine not having it. It really has shaped my personality and made me empathetic and understanding as well as more persistent and driven. I think I just want people to know that TS is just something I have, something that I am dealing with, and it is not the swearing disease. There is a lot more to it than that. We're all different, and we should all OWN IT!

Twiz 9

"The passenger living inside me"

No, not twizzler or twizzle, it's just Twiz. You might think, "What kind of name is that?" Well, it's a nickname of course. It kind of comes from a couple places. I was actually out the other night at a dinner party and someone asked me about it. I never know if I should go with the fact that I am a woman that looks so much like a man, or go with the route that I have Tourette syndrome and because of my twitches, I have turned into Twiz. Hi, I'm twitchy Liz, or Twiz. I start the conversation with, "I have Tourette syndrome." He replies with, "Nooooooo...you don't," which is his way of saying, "I figured." I have quite a few very visible tics, so his response doesn't bother me. I find it interesting to see how people approach other disorders, I was just relieved that I didn't have to educate him, but by the end of the night, I did have to educate his wife.

I'm thirty years old living in Brooklyn, NY. I guess you could say up to this point I have been a professional student, and I'm good at it. I have a collection of degrees including a master's in fine arts, a master's in art therapy, and I'm currently writing my thesis on TS. I would love to be an art therapists with my own practice, and even at some point become a teacher.

Growing up, my peers found my TS more interesting than the fact that my gender did not match my physical sex. It did help that I was fortunate enough to be with the same kids from pre-K to eighth grade. They all grew up with me, and knew me even before the tics started. I was about seven when I first started ticcing and I remember it was super scary. I couldn't help it, and I couldn't control it. It just happened. My parents couldn't tell me what was happening, and often put pressure on me to "stop it." It became very annoying very quickly; it just snuck up on me and exploded. It was like getting scared in a haunted house, quick and fast.

When I was about eight, I would often ask her what the feeling I was experiencing was, but she never had an answer. For the next year, my mother invested most of her time learning as much as she could about what was going on with me and the syndrome. She tried to learn as much as humanly possible, which was hard, especially seeing that this was before the Internet search engines were what they are today. My siblings would become annoyed and ask me to stop, and I was often not allowed to play with other children or my friends. It was very embarrassing, but I tried not to let it affect me that much, and I was somewhat of a loner anyways.

One day I was in the garage working on some drawings. The controlled focus of my childhood drawing seemed to help me not tic as much. My mother came into the garage and asked to talk to me. She sat me down and simply said, "You're going to be made fun of," and went on to explain why. She said that it was not my fault, and I could deal with it however I wanted to deal with it, but she gave me the courage to not feel badly about myself. She told me to be strong and that I can do anything, and the people who do have something to say are ignorant and uneducated. From that moment on, I felt very comfortable and open to talk about it with whomever. In fact, I found the more I talked about it, the more we all became comfortable with it. I was twelve years old when I went to my twin brother's therapist appointment, which he could not make, but it was already paid for. Within a few seconds, she had a book off the shelf and opened to TS. My mother screamed out, "I knew it!"

I was excited it had a name! I was relieved, but I also felt sad that it could not be fixed and that I would most likely have to live this way for the rest of my life. I did find comfort in the fact that there was a possibility of growing out of it, or at least a little bit. Unfortunately, I didn't; I still have it. My mother never told me what it was, just that I was going to be made fun of, so when I was officially diagnosed and my mother yelled out triumphantly, it made me a little mad. I had been asking and questioning these feeling for years. I think she was just too scared to say it aloud.

Even though I was diagnosed, my mother was hell bent to not medicate me. This wasn't an agreed decision with my father. My father wishes I had been put on medication or at least tried some out, especially on those hard days that it was difficult for me to complete tasks due to my tics. My mother's concern was mainly the side effect that they would cause. She swore to try every alternative treatment in the book instead.

My mother was very good at taking initiative and letting teachers and families know. I was lucky that most of my schools were small private schools, but I still had my problems. My kindergarten teacher was brutal, often yelling at me to stop and would call me a troublemaker. She would sit me in the corner, and restrict me from participating in game etc. In high school, I had a teacher that always reminded me that I had to complete all tasks despite the difficulties that might arise, which I believed. I later found out I was entitled to untimed or extended timed testing.

High school was my first taste of real bullying, and discrimination. I was bullied a bit in elementary school but it came on a lot harder in high school. That's when the explaining started. I'm the type of person to roll with the punches. I didn't always like advocating, or educating especially as a teen, but this is the time you are most worried about fitting in and want to fade into the masses. I was not given this luxury, so I went full throttle in the other direction, with a little encouragement from my mother and close friends. For a short time, I had help from my mother who made it quite clear I was going to struggle my whole life, especially in society. I thought, "Well, I better come to terms quick and figure out how I can use it for my own advantage."

One day in high school, during Friday's entire school meeting, I got up and addressed the entire school. I explained what TS was and why I did what I did. I also informed them that I was a very open person and they should feel free to approach me and ask any questions they had. I did this because I was just so sick of all the rumors and under-breath bullying. It was from this point on that I tried to embrace people's ignorance and just try to explain myself, which can be very hard to do. It took a lot of teenage courage to get up in front of your whole high school and address a topic that I had been bullied for, and do it with a positive outlook. I knew I could never fit in, or just fade to gray, but this might be the best way to relieve the stress from people talking about me behind my back. I got in a couple fights over students spreading rumors about me and asking my friend why they hung out with a "faggot freak" like me who twitches because I probably have some STD. Obviously, some people still could not be educated, and they wanted nothing to do with me.

I was lucky enough to have the support of my mother and close friends, if I didn't I know it would have been easy to lock myself in my house, secluding myself with my embarrassing tics. Don't get me wrong, at times, they have gotten the better of me, causing chaotic outbreaks of screaming and heaving and whatever else. Afterward, I do feel better, but unfortunately, one of these episodes can really clear a room. A good twenty-minute dose of hitting, twitching, sniffing, coughing, barking, smacking, gouging, and whatever else is a good release, as long as I can manage not bruising a rib. When I was young, I would walk on my toes everywhere, bark, hum, yelp, and squeak. As I got older, I stopped most of my vocal tics; I only sniff, sneeze, and cough. I've also figured out ways to disguise my tics, people often think its allergies.

Many people with TS deal with a variety of underlying conditions, including OCD, social anxiety disorder, and ADD to mention a few. As for me, I just really deal with my tics. I don't have enough symptoms to have a diagnosis of OCD, but my house does have to be neat, organized, and cleaned before I can focus on anything else. As for the social anxiety disorder, when I was younger, I think I worried what others would think of me, but I think that is just a part of growing up and our development process. Now I don't think I worry, but I definitely don't look forward to the daily struggle over who gets to control my body during different daily tasks. It or me? I definitely procrastinate doing certain things that I don't want to do, knowing it will be harder to suppress my tics.

I often consider my TS as a passenger living inside me, sharing my skin, two peas in a not-so-comfortable pod, trapped for eternity. It can be pretty annoying because it gets so crowded in here. For me, my TS is impossible to hide. For the most part, everyone notices. My girlfriend thinks my twitching is adorable, but she's also become used to it. She's told me that I don't tic in my sleep. "It's amazing that you don't move a wink when you're asleep," she told me. I told her that by the time I go to sleep, my body is too exhausted from ticcing all day to tic. It's a constant workout and my body just goes into complete relaxation mode.

When I wake up in the morning, I usually have about thirty minutes before BOOM, first tic of the morning to ya! I usually hope I get a few things done before I start—it sucks being on the toilet and having that first tic come and I end up peeing all over myself. "Good morning!" It usually happens when I'm brushing my teeth and I almost remove my tonsils with my toothbrush. I have a real convenient tic of slapping myself and gouging my left eye, so needless to say, manscaping can be dangerous. One time I removed half my eyebrow with a shaver. What a way to start the day.

As the day goes on, it's time to enter society. I find it easier to travel with a friend because I notice that people are less concerned with me when there is someone else with me. I figure they're thinking that I can't be on drugs or a crazy person because there is someone else with me, conversing with me, and they don't seem bothered by me. Actually, those are the only times when I receive the "understanding" smile, whatever the hell that means. It's as if people feel the need to nod to me when they understand it's a disorder, and that I am actually not a nuisance. I guess this is better than the stares, glares, and people yelling at me to cover my mouth, or "H1N1, asshole." With the stares and glares, I usually try to catch them in the act and smile at them, or point to my forearm where I have "TWITCH" tattooed. Usually this responsive behavior gets them to focus elsewhere. I even had some old ladies one time on a crowded subway lean over to me and say, "It would be more comfortable for everyone on the train if you didn't move so much," as if I was doing it for the purpose of looking cool.

I deal with prejudice in many ways. I've had cops follow me around stores, been asked to leave restaurants, and I've been refused service. I get a lot of grief from the DMV, but I have no problems. I didn't think I would be able to drive stick, or a motorcycle, but I have. Not sure how safe it is, but no one at the DMV could answer that. I've also had hard times getting hired for jobs because they think I can't do certain things due to my tics. One time I was interviewing at a candy store and after I explained I had TS, he asked me if I was aware that I would be working customer service. I thought, "How rude," especially seeing he was holding my resume which stated I worked customer service at a pharmacy for a year.

I guess I'm just still shocked by people's ignorance. One time I was stuck in the last row of a plane, right in front of the bathrooms. It was a flight from San Francisco to New York, so a nice long flight with a lot of people waiting in line to pee. This was just a bad day, and I was sick of smiling at every Tom, Dick, and Harry that stood there staring, waiting for confirmation of what they might have caught out of the corner of their eye. It's very hard to keep cool, controlled, and calm all the time; sometimes enough is enough. When I felt the heavy stares, I just yelled out," What? What are you staring at?" My arms reached out in that "I don't understand" position. "I have a neurological disorder. Please mind your own business. Would you stare at a paraplegic?" They would act as if they were doing no such thing and slowly look away. I try not to be this way, I'd rather educate in hopes that they will pass it along to someone else, but sometimes it's difficult to always be that person.

On the rare occasion, I will be among friends when someone decides they need to give me a piece of their mind. I was with friends at a sushi restaurant, having a great time with friends, when the man behind me rudely interrupted us asking me "if I minded." I explained to the man that I have TS and he was stuck at the table behind me. He exclaimed in disbelief, "Really? Really, come on! Really?" He then proceeded to call the hostess over asking that I be moved. The hostess seemed completely disgusted with the man's behavior and replied that all the tables were taken, and that he would have to deal. He made a fuss and left the restaurant. I'm not sure what his issue was, but I was glad to have the support of the restaurant.

It's not always that easy. One time I was at a bar in Miami and the bartender, who I was getting along with, asked me why I was twitching. I simply said, "I have Tourette," and showed her the "Twitch" tattoo on my arm. She went from all smiles to frowns and asked me to leave. I asked her for the reason and she ignored me. A regular at the bar said, "The lady asked you to go, no matter what the reason is." So I did. I told my friend who was smoking a cigarette outside, who stormed in, explaining to her that I do have TS and that it is fucked up to ask me to leave. She eventually gave in to her disbelief and came outside. She told me I was fucked up for making fun of people with TS and that her younger brother had TS. I replied to her story with all respect, telling her that I loved her passion in supporting the cause and her family member, but that she needs to not be ignorant to the rest of the world who may also have TS. I explained that I truly did have TS, but she refused to believe me. It was really the oddest thing.

One time I had a three-hour layover in Rhode Island before heading back to San Francisco. I figured I would get a beer while waiting.

The bartender served me after thoroughly checking my ID, because remember, I look like a nineteen-year-old boy. When I was ready for my second beer, she said she did not feel comfortable. I asked why, and she said she did not have to serve me if she did not want to. At first I thought I'd better leave the situation, but then I thought, "No, actually." I asked to speak with the manager. She sent him to me and he asked me, "What is the problem, sir?" I said, "Actually, it's Ms. and if that's why she won't serve me a drink then that is a big problem, and I could sue the bar." Then I asked him the same question, "Why won't she serve me?" I said, "With all due respect, I will leave the bar, but if she is refusing me because of my appearance, or my sexual orientation, then we have a problem. And if she is refusing me service because of my neurological disorder, then that is plain ignorant. And if she was worried or curious, she should have asked." I was nothing but polite to her and the manager. I looked around the bar and pointed out a man in a wheelchair and a black man, and asked if she was not serving them as well. I proceeded to look at my watch. I noticed it was after noon, and I said to him, "Do I look like a junkie? Is it seven thirty in the morning and I'm shaking through withdrawals and I need a fix somehow before I get on this plane?" I asked him if he would serve me, and then politely asked him to let his bartender know what I had told him. He proceeded to serve me and informed me that she still did not feel comfortable serving me, but I believe she was just embarrassed at that point. Nevertheless, I didn't have to pay the tab.

I understand in this society that things are a certain way, and I am definitely not the norm. I can get annoyed and sad, mad at times, or feel defeated. These are all things I am doing to myself. Therefore, I am constantly reminding myself that what doesn't kill me makes me stronger, and I try to excel through life, not worried about the little things. I remind myself that things could be much worse. I remind myself that people just don't understand, and that I have the power to educate. Having TS has made me able to speak up, even if I don't want to, but I have to, my disorder is in your face.

I still don't feel comfortable being an everyday educator on the subject, even though it can be ever so repetitive, but with the support of friends and family and therapy and art making, I find it is becoming easier. In addition, the more others know about the disorder, hopefully the easier it will be for those young kids who have been diagnosed to feel comfortable and confident in their bodies and be able to live a great and fulfilling life. I think TS has made me stronger in many ways. I do not think I would be the same person I am today without the TS; however, it would be nice to be able to kick off my shoes, watch a movie, and not move, at least for a minute. I cannot even imagine how that must feel. I do not think TS is what defines me, but it is all part of me, well, more like existing next to me, like a parasite. We all have to deal with what life brings us. Sometimes, I'd like to smack the face off some people's heads for not giving me a second to just exist, quietly. I try to find the positive in everything.

You can't live through life feeling defeated or you will never get anything done. Unfortunately, many children with TS often feel defeated from an early age. Despite what life has doled to you, no matter who you are, no one said it was going to be easy, actually, my mother told me it was going to be rip raging difficult. Without that kind of tough love, I wouldn't be here today. I continue to educate, and I continue to be open to everyone I cross paths with. And when

I see someone on a train, I don't stare, even if they're merely having a psychotic episode or just sneezing.

I understand life from a different perspective. I understand struggle, and I am humbled by the life I was given and I can see things and be thankful for things that I have, that others don't, and vice versa. I wish strangers were more aware of the disorder, and I wish they understood that it's not just all curse words, but also, the fact that TS is not what I represent. I am also an artist, a learner, a worker, etc. It does not define me.

Aman 10

"If you can have self-confidence, no one can take that away from you"

My name is Aman. I'm thirty years old and I work as a financial professional. I work in the areas of financial advisory (mergers and acquisitions, specifically) and principal investing. I am currently living in NYC, but I am originally from Delhi, India, where non-debilitating diseases and syndromes like Tourette syndrome are not giving much interest. I first started having tics around thirteen years old, but was not officially diagnosed until I was twenty-six years old.

I had no discernible tics as a pre-teen; my tics started developing around thirteen years old. At first, they were semi-mild, but around seventeen or eighteen, they got progressively worse. Never having heard of TS, and me being a little older when I started really having issues with my tics, I was more confused than anything else. I was embarrassed by them, and I always invented some story for why I was ticcing. To most people, I said it was some type of sports injury with my various shoulder tics. My facial grimacing tic didn't start until I was around nineteen or twenty years old. This is when the real embarrassment and stress started. I still had not been diagnosed, my family doctor thought I was hyperactive or had OCD.

My tics started simply with shoulder jerks and hand gestures. They have since morphed into complex tics, full-body, complex movements, often accompanied by coughs and throat clearing. Since most of my tics were fairly simple during my school years, I never had to deal with too much teasing or bullying. I escaped the most immature phases of my life without TS. For the most part, if someone did ask me, I would play it off as a sports injury, my T-shirt was too tight, I was claustrophobic, or I just had the hiccups. Because of the simplicity of my tics, most kids were polite when asking me if something was wrong.

When I hit adolescence and my body started to change, I started developing tics. I just started having unexplained body movements. Not knowing what it was made it less scary. I just thought it was something I was doing and that I wasn't hurting myself. My parents sent me to a couple doctors, who didn't see any concern and didn't recommend any test. One doctor had me sit still for five minutes, which I was able to do. I knew I could suppress whatever was going on in my body, but they didn't know I was suppressing the tics. The doctor told my parents that I was just going through changes, and I could stop if I wanted to.

High school was quite difficult for me. It's the time you start meeting girls, but my tics weren't that bad. I didn't have any facial tics yet. I think facial tics and complex tics are the worst, because if it's a body tic, you can disguise it more than you can with a facial tic. Facial tics you can see; you can't hide a facial tic. I didn't have the facial tics yet but I had the body tics, and they would rapidly morph into other tics. One day I would have one where I would shack my head, the next day I would be contorting my back and the next day slapping myself. It was morphing all the time. I thought I was being weird. When I was in public, I would try my hardest to control it, but when I was in private, I would tic away.

In school, I was very athletic, sort of a jock type. Being a jock and getting into sports helped with my self-confidence and I had many friends. When I did any type of sports, I never did any of my tics, but in class was a different story. I thought I was restless, but I didn't really understand. When I was in class, I was clearly uncomfortable. I would shake my desk all the time and the teacher would ask me what's going on. I would just apologize and try to move on.

I met my future wife in high school. When we first met, she asked me what was wrong. I just said I was uncomfortable all the time, and she just dealt with it. When I was alone with her, she would ask me to stop. Neither of us knew what was wrong with me, so she would ask me if I was able to stop, I told her I think so. She said to concentrate and try to stop. She would challenge me to try to stop, and said it was an unattractive quality, which was hurtful because the fact was that I just couldn't stop. For the most part, she has been nothing but supportive. She has been a large reason I have been able to get through this. Having the love of your life stand by you through all of this can really help you get through many situations.

My wife was a rock on the outside, but insecure on the inside. She would never let anybody make fun of me, constantly telling people there was nothing wrong with me. If her parents asked what was wrong, she would say, "What do you mean? There's nothing wrong with him." I could tell she was embarrassed, especially in public when I was shaking my head, but she has always stood by my side.

I went to college in the US, which is vastly different from India. By this point, the facial grimacing had started and the head shaking got worse. I would have more complex tics, which combined the facial tics with the body tics. I also started more verbal tics, where I was clearing my throat a lot more, and the OCD started too. It was the continuous cycle of people asking me, "What's wrong," and me just saying the same patterns of excuses: "I have a sports injury," "My leg hurts," or, "I have the hiccups." The hiccups excuse was not a good one because it ended up causing me to have a hiccup tic.

I made an entirely new set of friends and many of the new people I encountered teased me about my tics. People would imitate my tics, and make fun of me; sometimes my friends would do it too. Still undiagnosed, I would just play along. I've always been a fairly confident, outgoing person, so I tried not letting it bother me too much. I was just like, "I'm doing it, but I have no idea what's going on." I just dealt with it. I would make myself stop from time to time, and I just thought it was a bad habit that I had to stop, and thought I had to break the habit. I just needed to make myself stop. I still had no idea it was TS, so I just kept on living. People in the US were more open about making fun of you for things. It was hard. I even got made fun of by my roommates. They eventually saw through it and realized I was a nice person.

In 2005, I started working at in investment banking job, and I was working a hundred-hour weeks. The combination of having TS, all the work, OCD, ADHD, no diagnosis, and no medication was hard. It created a soup of tics. We were in a grown-up stage now. Now people wouldn't make fun of me. They would just ask if I was all right, and I would tell them yes and just do the best work I could. However, I was really starting to wonder about what was going on. The more tired I would get, the more complex and violent the tics would get. I knew something was off, but I just continued with my excuses; sports injuries, hiccups, etc. People would say, "Are you okay?" And I would say, "Yeah, why?" They would say, "You just moved." I would say, "No, I didn't." They would just roll their eyes and not ask again. I guess I just stopped trusting people. I didn't trust if I said to someone, "I just don't know what's wrong. I don't know why I do this, and I don't think I can stop." I didn't think they would understand, and I wasn't sure if I really wanted to tell myself that.

Around this time, I came across a blog by a girl with TS describing her tics. It mirrored myself so much that I e-mailed her. She put me in contact with someone at the TSA, who I met with and she told me I probably did have Tourette syndrome. This was the first time that I heard this in regard to me. Up until this point, I thought TS was what they said in the media, a bunch of yelling and screaming obscenities. I started reading up more on the condition, found a doctor at NYU, and received my official diagnosis of TS. She put me on a small dosage of Klonopin, and I've been on it ever since. I never want to up the dosage because I never want to use it as a crutch.

I think the diagnosis was such a relief. It was a complete change in my attitude. I thought that since now I knew what was wrong with me, I could go out and tell people what it was, and that it was something I can't stop. It's something that I have, but it has not held me back. It was just a relief to put a name to a condition that I feared could be a lot worse. I finally had a name to attach to my body movements. The years spent wondering what exactly was wrong with me melted away.

My parents, who still live in India, never really thought anything was wrong with me, and still don't really acknowledge it, but my girlfriend, now wife probably had the hardest time dealing with it. However, she did cope with it admirably. She knows that the chances of our children developing it are high, but has never once tried to suggest that it is an issue that weighs on her mind. It does weigh on my mind, a lot.

Since I wasn't diagnosed until after college, I was never able to explain myself to my peers. The time that I would have to discuss it with my peers was at work. I had tons of trepidation before I could finally admit or describe my TS to my colleagues. I knew working in a highly charged, mostly male environment would come with tons of off-color humor. The unfortunate comedic media portrayal of TS did nothing to help my fear in addressing my colleagues and friends. However, when I finally did admit it, everyone was very understanding and supportive. It was a huge burden off my shoulders. I now feel more relaxed at work and at ease with my condition. I make it a point to let new colleagues know I have TS and that I'm not ashamed of it. That lets them know that I don't consider myself deficient because of it. I am often thankful that by the time I was diagnosed I was old enough to have the courage and self-confidence to address my colleagues without too much concern. Honestly, it was a non-issue to most of my colleagues and friends. None of them really saw me as deficient—I let them know in a matter of fact way to confirm that I felt exactly the same. I was able to tell people what was wrong with me when they asked, and I started trusting people more. I told them, "I have TS," and they would say, "Oh, okay" and we would move on. TS has made me more compassionate, more understanding, more believing in people and that's a great quality to have. If I didn't have TS, maybe I'd be more cynical, so what a blessing it is to have TS.

Over time, I've developed mild forms (in my opinion) of ADD and OCD. With my OCD, I don't have any specific hygiene-related compulsions, but I constantly get stuck repeating words. I feel compelled to read aloud often, even when there are others around. If a word has the letter *f* or *v* in it, I need to repeat the word constantly until it feels right. I want to repeat aloud what I hear on TV. I am also often compelled to touch sharp objects. It takes considerable effort to stave off these feelings. As for my ADD, it causes me to be constantly and easily distracted. I'm an outgoing, gregarious person anyway, so the ADD really doesn't help, but I can deal with the ADD when I have to. I also have severe claustrophobia because of my TS. I once had to endure an MRI and the confined space and the inability to move was EXCRUCIATING. It's the OCD and the facial/vocal tics that I wish would just go away.

After I was diagnosed, I went on to go to business school. This was a more professional setting, not like college. I thought about reinventing myself, this was a chance to wipe the slate clean, but I said, "I'm not going to change." I'm just going to be who I am, myself. I was very open about my TS; if people asked, I told them. My then-girlfriend was afraid of how open I was. I would tell people that didn't even ask because I wanted to set the tone early. I didn't want people to think something was wrong with me, because I didn't believe something was wrong with me. It was as much a part of me as my name or where I was from. Everyone was very supportive and understanding.

I tic a lot, but there are things that make me tic worse, speaking in public, confined spaces, lack of sleep, stress, being around others who tic. I know my tics are worse late at night, when my Klonopin has worn off and I'm more tired. My brain is tired from fighting TS every day, but it's another day in the book, and I still get to come home to a loving, supportive wife. When I get home, I just try to relax. I'll watch television, spend time with my wife and puppy, read, or have some wine. I do drink socially, so I drink often, but very much in moderation. It doesn't make my tics any worse, but it does make me think I'm a better dancer than I really am!

My TS causes me to be tired, but to be honest, I don't know what life would be like without my TS. Perhaps I wouldn't be as conscious as I am while meeting new people. As a young adult, I couldn't explain what I was doing and when people made fun of me, I would just laugh it off. I just kept a positive attitude and went on living my life. Over time, I have become very open about it. I feel it will be educational to those around me, and it allows me not to worry about what others might think. I know my children will likely inherit the condition and that is certainly a curse, however, it is a part of who I am. Having TS gives me the opportunity to give back to the TS community, to help teens believe that TS shouldn't hold them back. TS will not put any dreams out of reach. In that regard, it is a blessing to me. It's hard to understand TS, people just do not understand it. If you have it, no explanation is necessary. If you don't have it, no explanation is sufficient. TS has never held me back from achieving anything. I don't blame TS for anything. It is not a disability. It is a condition that has to be dealt with. I try to maintain a confident, outgoing demeanor and this helps me deal with my TS better than any medicine.

I want to set an example for everyone with TS. This is not a disability; it's a syndrome. That's my attitude that I use every day. I used to try to suppress my tics on a daily basis, now I only do it when I'm in a meeting or interview where I think it might make people uncomfortable. I really want to bring a message of love and confidence. If you can have self-confidence, no one can take that away from you, and that confidence will shine through every single day in everything you do. We are creative, smart, driven people and we can do whatever we want to do. The first step is self-realization. Again, it's not a disability and we can't use it as a crutch. Put you best foot forward. TS has given me so many negative things, but it has given me a positive attitude.

Jesse 11

"Same on the inside"

My name is Jesse. I'm thirty-three years old originally from Saint Joseph, Missouri. I now live in New Bedford, Massachusetts. I've lived in New Bedford for about four years now and currently working as an ophthalmic medical assistant, and I am going to New Bedford University for psychology. I really love helping people, and I believe that's why I'm here. Whether it's helping people see or helping with psychological issues, I just want to help. I really think this need to help stems from my Tourette syndrome. I know what I have gone through and been put through in life and I hate to see others go through the same. I first noticed my tics in about fifth or sixth grade. Originally, I had a head twitch/roll and a facial eye twitch.

I graduated from a Catholic high school in 1996. I attended Catholic school for most of my educational years. In school, I had only a few friends. The friends I did have had their own various flaws. Outside of school, I cannot honestly remember if I had any symptoms around them. If I did, they just never said anything about it that stuck in my mind. We just never discussed them.

I never really realized I had a problem or that I was different until my classmates started teasing me. My classmates are the reason I found out about my TS. They did not know why I had tics; they just knew I was different. I was always the quiet kid in class. I still kind of am. I was repeatedly picked on and teased, which led me to search for the reason behind my head and facial tics.

The kids would stand in front of me and shake their heads when I had a tic, then laugh at me constantly. I know they had names for me, but I can't really remember what they were, or I blocked them out. I became quite isolated throughout grade school and high school. I was very scared and embarrassed due to the unceasing mockery. When the other kids would realize their taunting was bothering me, they did it even more. It was always hard to go to school, because I knew what the day was going to bring: the relentless picking on and mocking for my tics. And the worst thing of it was that there was not much support by the teachers. Throughout my school history, I don't recall any teacher doing much to defend me or educate the other children.

This went on even after I was diagnosed. I hoped that telling them what it was that was causing the unusual tics, they would make them stop harassing me. When I did discover it was TS, it did not stop them. They didn't seem to care. Quite similar to the kids in school, I was mocked by my father. Whenever I would tic, he would imitate me and shake his head. He would mock me when I was doing my homework, at the dinner table, getting ready for school, or just around the house. I am not sure exactly how long this went on for, but unlike the teachers at school, my mother quickly put an end to that. At school, the teachers were not always as shielding. I don't hold a grudge, especially with the children. Kids are going to be kids! I have had one person apologize for their behavior in school, but I'm sure the rest of them don't even realize they did anything wrong. They didn't understand what they were doing, or don't want to say anything about it now. I don't put too much thought into it.

I forgive them. For me personally, I don't think our grade school years are what completely define us as people. Don't get me wrong, it definitely did make for a hard time. I often wonder if these years fed into my social anxiety disorder, making me the way I am now, or if this is just how the TS makes me.

I guess I was finally relieved when I had a diagnosis. Now I just had to play the roller coaster of medication trials. The first doctor I went to was in Saint Joseph, Missouri. He was the doctor to give me the official diagnosis. Since then I have only seen a few doctors for TS, and I don't discuss it very much with my GP (general practitioner). I have found that most doctors know as much about TS as some random person on the street. This uninformed mentality has me a bit concerned. I had one doctor attempt to treat me with nicotine. He said it would help control the tics. Seeing that I don't smoke, I attempted to chew nicotine gum. I did not try this method very long as I did not see much difference in my tic, and frankly I found the taste disgusting. I've just been on so many medications but not many have worked, or they cause almost unbearable side effects. I was on Prozac, Haldol, and Buspirone to name a few. I find that the Buspirone helps the most with my anxiety; the others really seemed to affect my personality and cloud my mind.

Along with my TS I have an underlying condition of anxiety disorder, mine is mostly social. When I was a child, I did have a doctor diagnose me with mild OCD; however, I am not aware of any symptoms. At the time, I was already diagnosed with TS, and after discussing symptoms I was experiencing, my GP added OCD to my diagnosis. I would repeatedly check that I did things, such as set my alarm clock at night. I still believe this has more to do with the fact that I so often forgot to do it rather than some type of OCD quality. As a child, I cannot say I was a very organized individual, but I did not like getting dirty at all! However, now I can say that I do like things to be straight and organized. I can get agitated with little thing, such as boxes of cereal not on the shelf neatly. Is it OCD or just adulthood?

As you can see, it seemed that the doctors were as confused as I was, and not too informative. So when I was diagnosed, it made it a tad difficult to try and explain to my classmates, so I started spending a lot of time alone. I distanced myself from people and learned to enjoy the company of myself. I continued this even after school. I was just annoyed with people and their mentalities. I became rebellious. I put on this tough guy facade so people wouldn't bother me. I wanted them to fear me. I was out of school, away from all those classmates that picked on me for so many years, and I was on my own. I was alone, and I put all the school years behind me. I like it, being alone. In fact, I even looked for jobs that I would be alone or by myself. I worked as a security officer where I worked alone, then I was a delivery driver for a bank, also alone. I did work as a driver for Brinks armored car and I did have a partner, but after that, I went back on the road alone as a semi-truck driver.

I did finally grow out of the working alone phase, and started being a little more social, but I am still trying to keep it minimal. I have been working as an ophthalmic medical assistant. I perform medical exams and testing for a corneal specialist. I also fit contacts for the practice, so I deal with patients all day. Between the isolation jobs and now being an OMA, I have had many interesting jobs. I just didn't want my TS to keep me from living my life, or let me try new things. I was a volunteer fire fighter and a licensed EMT (Emergency Medical Technician.) Working with the fire department and being an EMT, I was placed in many stressful situations, but the anxiety didn't get to me. It was actually like I had no anxiety. I could lead a team into a fire or perform an extraction with the Jaws of Life with a steady hand and mind.

It was great; we were all like a family. I don't know if anyone knew I had TS, I never really brought it up unless asked. With my TS, I don't initiate the conversation. I like to think that people don't notice the tics, even though they are very frequent and constant. Sometimes I can suppress them but I feel it boiling and boiling inside of me until I just pop and a tic comes out. The whole build-up process could last just a few seconds or it might wax and wane for a few minutes, but no matter what, it will come out.

After working as an EMT is when I merged my career into ophthalmology and became a certified optician. This brought on a whole new venture in my life. I started working in an ophthalmologist office in Holts, Missouri, for a doctor. He was a great doctor who I really looked up to. He often had to travel for work-related events, meetings, seminar, etc., and he would take me with him. He owned his own plane so we would often fly. It was a small plane, probably seated about eight people. After a while of working and traveling with him, he started to teach me to fly the plane. I soon went off to get my private pilot's license. I would often rent planes and go for day trips. I was great.

It was soon after that when I met my now wife, Jennifer. She was originally from the east coast, Massachusetts area, and we decided to leave and move east. When we first moved to New Bedford, we lived near the center of town. It was much louder and busier there and was not good for my anxiety issues. My wife is very understanding of my anxiety and now we are on the outskirts of town. A nice quiet building that looks out on trees and a park. I like quiet, secluded places more; I'm just kinda used to it. When I bought my first house back in Holts, it was on a large piece of land. It was set back with a little pond, not to close to neighbors. I never really had to deal with my neighbors, or wanted to. I guess it just helped me keep to myself. It's not exactly that I want to be alone, or that I don't want to hang out with people, because I do. I wish I could go out and be more social, I'd like to be more social. It's just that my anxiety hits when I'm in large groups of people, especially large groups of people I don't know. I just try to avoid those situations the best I can.

My wife is a big Red Sox fan and despite the crowds, I have accompanied her to games. It's hard with the crowds, but I have come up with a little trick to help me deal. I bring my camera and watch the game through the camera lens. It makes me feel like I'm the only one there. My wife is such a huge Red Sox fan that it was always her dream to get married in Fenway Park, so we did. On August 3, 2010, right before the opening pitch for the Red Sox versus the Indians game, we were married in the stands. This was me helping her fulfill her dream. Thankfully, the Red Sox won, otherwise it might have been perceived as a bad omen.

With the lack of a big social life, we spend a lot of time at home, especially in the winter. I'm not a big winter person; I like the summer a lot more. I love water and nature, fishing, kayaking, biking, outdoor stuff. So when winter does hit, I tend to hibernate. Sometimes we will have a couple of friends over, but I don't really do the bar or club thing.

I don't have many close friends, but my closest friend is my priest. After high school, I fell away from the church, but this year I felt a calling to come back. I'm actually looking to become a third order

Carmelite through the lay, and become a deacon at the church. I go to church every week, but I try to get there early so I can get a seat and be there before the crowds roll in. No one at the church knows I have TS except for the priest. It is hard to hide it or hold it in during mass, and I feel like the more people there are the more tics I have. I can often give myself tension headaches by trying to control my tics, my anxiety only make it worse. When I'm anxious, my tics become more rapid which makes me try harder to control them. It's a vicious circle. The fear of people seeing my uncontrollable tics leads to the increased anxiety. I'm paranoid that people will criticize me if they notice my tics.

With my recent reconnection to the church, I decided to get married again in a church. Even though we were married civilly, we had not received the sacrament of marriage. The Catholic Church views marriage as a vocation, and receiving this sacrament brought us closer to the church.

I'm in school right now for psychology, and I'd like to do one on one, or even some type of support group in conjunction with the church. I still want to work as an ophthalmologist, and just do psychology as a part time thing. No matter what I do, I just want to continue helping others in whatever way I can. Right now, I am volunteering for an organization that I work one on one with a person with a mental illness. Ironically, the person I am working with suffers from severe anxiety, much higher than mine. It's nice because I can relate to him. We can talk freely because we understand each other. If we're out and he's not comfortable, I understand. That's the thing, if I'm out with my wife and I get uncomfortable, she doesn't understand completely. She just can't relate.

A day in my life can be a struggle, but I push on. My tics start pretty much as soon as I wake up, with the vocal tics coming on in the late morning. Usually the first thing I do is my morning prayer. I've heard a lot of people with TS try different things to help control their tics, like prayer and meditation, but it doesn't work for me. Over the years, my tics have gotten worse. As a kid, I had head and eye tics, now I also have a cough tic, and an arm flex. My symptoms were only part time as a kid, now they are pretty constant.

With my cough tic, my patients think I am coughing or laughing, and sometimes I have to explain it to them. I have had a few patients with TS and I try to discuss it with them, but I have found that they don't want to discuss it. I can completely understand this, most of the time I don't want to discuss it either. I often wonder what medical treatments are out there now for TS. I haven't seen a doctor who specializes in TS in years and would like to one day, but with my wife currently unemployed and me working and in school, our financial situation is a little tight right now. The economy isn't helping out that much either.

It is concerning to me because I know my tics get worse after a hard day at work, crowded situations, or even congested driving situations. The increased tics mean increased anxiety. If it is a hard day at work I try to suppress my tics when I'm with patients, then they just come out vocally as my cough. I think the cough one is the one I worry about the most. There have been times when I'm trying to eat, and a vocal tic comes out causing me to choke. It's pretty scary, and always makes me think of future. I'm afraid of being an old man and choking because of a tic. Along with the cough tic, my arm flexing makes me wonder too. Earlier this year, the flex was quite expensive and caused fatigue in my arm, and my arm really hurt for a while.

The time when I feel the most peace is when I'm asleep. Every night before I go to bed I do my evening prayer. I might play some video game, or play on Facebook before I go to sleep. It helps me unwind from my day. When I do go to sleep, my wife knows when I am actually asleep because I stop ticcing.

No matter what, I feel I'm blessed with what I've done and who I am. I'm very satisfied, and wouldn't change a lot, even with having TS. It helps keep me grounded and humble. It reminds me to treat people how I would want to be treated. We're all the same inside. Despite having TS, I have perfectly normal cognitive abilities. I have been able to achieve anything I have set out to do. The only problem I have results from not being accepted by my classmates in grade school. It is important for children to know that just because someone is different in appearance, we are all the same on the inside. I believe God is up there watching us and we are only given what we can handle. I wouldn't wish TS on any one, but I am glad I was given it, something to make me humble and allow me to suffer.

Julie 12

"I've had a glimpse at the ugly side of humanity"

My name is Julie. I'm a thirty-three-year-old, fashion editor in NYC. I lived in Taiwan until I was about a year old before we moved around the Midwest until we finally settled outside the Boston area when I was in third grade. Up until this point, I had a pretty happy childhood, but when we moved to the Boston area, I felt lonely. All the other places we lived were suburban areas, but this new area was different. We were in a small neighborhood surrounded by nothing but busy roads, and there were not many kids my age, it was very isolating. It did not have that community feeling. Socially, it was different. The kids were different, and they were very clicky. It felt like all of a sudden I was not doing the right thing or wearing the right clothes.

I first noticed having a blinking tic when I was in first grade, even though my parents said they noticed it when I was a toddler. I never found the eye blinking too distracting. It wasn't until I was in fourth grade that I remember having the feeling that something was wrong with me from the neck up. I already had an obnoxious personality, and now the tics were becoming more pronounced. I started experiencing a lot of eye blinking, head jerking, and some facial grimacing, but it wasn't anything too crazy that anyone noticed except for me. It was annoying; it was like an itch that needed to be scratched, in a mental and a physical way, but I couldn't pinpoint where the itch was. From this point on, the tics started becoming more distracting to my speech, my physical actions, and my focus.

My parents took me to the doctor when I was in first grade for the blinking. He said it was probably just nerves from starting school, and that I just needed some love. My parents grew up in Taiwan in the '50s and '60s. I feel like they're from a different planet. They think everything can be solved with self-will and enough discipline. For a long time, they thought TS could be fixed. If I tried hard enough to stop it, it would go away. It was quite disheartening. Just fix it, and it will go way.

By the time I got into high school, the tics had become even worse. When I was in ninth grade, a couple friends and I went to the movies to see the *Twin Peaks* movie. I don't know why for some reason after that I started a snorting tic. This one is intense; I do a heavy snort and rub my nose. The snorting tic is my number one tic. That's the one that everyone notices and has still never gone away. For years, everyone thought I had allergies or a drug problem. Ironically, I did have allergies, and a drug problem, but my problem was not with coke. My mother took me to the doctor for an allergy shot thinking that it would help, it didn't. I went to school with the same people for years, so I guess they just got used to it, but that didn't mean the rumors didn't start. The snorting tic became worse as time went on and people generally assumed I was using cocaine, which was not a pleasant reputation to shoulder.

I always knew something was "off," but it never had a name until I read a magazine article that mentioned symptoms of TS when I was seventeen. I never really told anyone until I was halfway through college, but I also wasn't properly diagnosed until I was twenty. Up until that point, when anyone asked about my snorting, I would pretend not to hear them, or I would change the subject. When I was twenty years old, I went for a psychiatric evaluation where I was correctly diagnosed with TS. I was so happy I finally had a diagnosis. It was a great relief to give that "irritable feeling" a proper name. There was an explanation behind my snorting, head jerking, and screeching! It was nice to know I wasn't going crazy!

I did fairly well in school, well until the drug and alcohol abuse started. I always had a good relationship with my teachers. I never had a problem with any teachers until a few years after college. I was trying to get my transcript and the school told me there was an issue with the transcript. They had found that I was short credits needed to graduate. In order to get my transcript and diploma, I had to take a class for the missing credits. I took the class in my mid-twenties and had a very cranky teacher. By this point, I had developed a tic with paper; I had to crinkle it to turn the page, and it made a lot of noise. This annoyed the teacher and drove her crazy. She would always say, "Can you stop that!" I explained to her why I was doing this, but she would just say, "Well, try to stop it!" I guess with how noticeable my tics are I'm fortunate that this was the only problem that I ever had.

Throughout my TS, I have had a variety of tics, including head jerking, half body turns, shoulder shrugging, blinking, snorting, touching my face a lot, a lot of touching objects, toe scrunching, and awkward posing. It can get quite distracting. I also deal with OCD, ADD, and general anxiety disorder. I didn't realize or admit to the extent of these other disorders until I was nearly thirty years old. I didn't really think I was OCD because I didn't have the more widely publicized symptoms, counting, checking, and things like that. My

OCDs are more related to having difficulty transitioning from one task to another. I'll be overwhelmed with a feeling that something is missing, and then I have to start adding all these other random, extra things to do before I feel that the original task is complete. It's all these little tasks that add up—checking one more website, putting on more makeup, etc.

There's always something that can hold you back, especially when you're dealing with something like TS. I used to let dating hold me back, a lot. Dating was somewhat horrible for me, well not horrible, but a big source of fear for me for a long time. I just started talking about that in therapy in my twenties. It's been many years of work and facing my fears due to my tics, rejection, and anxiety. In middle school, when all my friends started entering the dating world, I could not grasp the strength to join in. I felt weird and a high fear of rejection, especially after my vocal tics started. In my twenties, I had a few short relationships, but after about six weeks, I would freak out and end it. I could never progress past that six-week point. I was out of touch with myself because I could not deal with having TS, and the issues I had with anxiety and alcoholism. I was never able to talk about my feelings or the other person's feelings. I didn't know what I wanted, so I would quickly end the relationship before it got to the point where we would have the "serious relationship" conversation.

In my thirties, I did start dating on a more serious level and it has actually been a pretty positive experience. I have done a lot of work in therapy, which has helped me break out of my shell. By then I started feeling normal about having TS. I used to be ashamed, afraid, and afraid of what people would think. I don't have those concerns anymore, and a lot less fear. Now I'm pretty open, and up front about my TS. Eventually they'll see my tics and the topic will come up.

As for my work setting, I have found people are quite empathetic and understanding to TS. Now in my life I'm very open. No one's shared this with me, but I'm sure it just makes them feel better to have some sort of explanation for behavior they couldn't understand at first glance. This is also the outcome of therapy. It just helped me to get to know the real me, and not the disorders. About two years after therapy, I began volunteering at the TSA in NYC. I began forcing myself to talk about who I was and my TS, instead of ignoring it or letting people assume that I was on cocaine. I finally started coming out of my little shell of denial and avoidance. It felt terrible, but I knew two things: people are going to be as comfortable with you as you are with yourself, and most new things are difficult, so you have to practice if you're ever going to get better. I was irrationally ashamed and embarrassed by my tics, but I knew if I let that spill over into my conversations with people about TS, they would get the assumption that this is a disorder that is shameful and embarrassing. I had to pretend having TS was no big deal, something I was completely okay with, until one day I really was okay with it. It seems almost ridiculous that I ever felt so freaked out to tell another person I have TS. Now it's like second nature to me, and I feel no need to apologize anymore for my condition.

I think getting sober also was a very crucial step for me coming to terms with my TS. When I drank, I found my tics got worse, and then decreased below normal levels when I had a hangover. I didn't care about my ticcing; it was just not a worry for me. I was convinced that the drinking would help my tics. I guess it did because I just didn't care what was going on with me. It just made it tolerable. It was the same outcome when I smoked pot. My friends would often tell me smoking made my tics worse, which I guess makes sense since they're both stimulants, but I didn't care, it just made me feel better.

During my drinking, I was prescribed Klonopin, but I didn't feel it helped that much; however, I was drinking and smoking a lot of pot, so they weren't working together. I would always say that the Klonopin would make my tics worse, even though it was more likely the alcohol and pot, but they were fun to drink with. I can't take them anymore because it did turn into an abusive situation. Now I'm at the point that I feel anything I do to screw with my system will do just that, screw up my system. I like to feel Zen, even-headed; I don't want anything in my body that brings me up or down.

It seems for many with TS that their tics got better in adulthood. Mine actually got a lot worse in high school and then a little better in adulthood, but it is definitely a lot worse now. My vocal tics are generally the same, and I've had the troublesome snorting tic for twenty years now. It's been much of the same muscle groups that do the ticcing. There hasn't been a lot of change, just some minor variation.

I have to be honest; I have let my TS hold me back from doing things. I've been afraid to go to job interviews before, even when I would have been considered prestigious in my field. I have also been afraid of dating. I've done a lot of work to heal myself, but I've long been petrified of men, dating, and people because I have felt so self-conscious about my tics.

I'm very aware of how my TS manifests. I know that loud, crowded places and confined spaces trigger my tics. Also, hunger, fatigue, and sitting in the same place for too long, so I try to avoid these situations, but that's not always the answer. I know that by the end of the day, my tics get worse, but there's no way to avoid the end of the day. I find what helps keep my tics manageable is regularity of lifestyle. I make sure to eat when I'm hungry, get lots of sleep and exercise. I try to exercise three times a week, and I find that it's stabilizing and helpful. It's a good release of energy. Sleep is probably the most important part of the equation, since fatigue exacerbates my tics quite a bit. With the increase of tics at the end of the day, I know the best thing to do is relax, and watch some TV. I hardly tic when I watch TV, and it's wonderful to just shut off for an hour or so at the end of the day.

With my sobriety, it's hard to find a medication that I feel okay to take and that works. Once I did try vitamin therapy. It was a crazy and expensive concoction of calcium, magnesium, fish oil, and some other thing. It didn't do too much for my tics, but I hardly got sick during that experiment. At one point, my doctor had me try Tenex, which is a high blood pressure medication that is used off label for TS. It helped very minimally, but had some side effects. I also tried Lexapro for the anxiety disorder, which helped bring down the tics a little bit, but not that much. My doctor has suggested other medications, but I have just been too fearful to try more powerful drug, such as anti-psychotics and anti-seizure medications. Sometimes it feels like a lost cause.

I rarely tic when I'm at home, but once I leave it's like tic city. This leads to a lot of anger; anger that I experience when someone else directs their anger at my tics, toward me. I have to deal with the reactions like weird looks, laughing, and downright abusive language at a high decibel directed at my TS. People's ignorance really affects me. I think someone not afflicted with TS would be surprised at how tiring it can be to tic, trying to suppress tics, and trying to refocus on what you were doing because of ticcing.

Ignorance is a big thing that I deal with. You would not believe how many grown adults out there will point, laugh, and speak about me as if I'm not there. They call me pig and make snorting noise at me mocking my tics. I don't know why, but my snorting tic offends strangers. They will confront me at a store, on the street, in the subway, or just anywhere. I explain to them that I have TS, and why I'm doing what I'm doing, and why I'm making these sounds. They still say that I'm disgusting and to use a tissue, or go to the bathroom. It's just really hard on my emotional well-being to constantly deal with all of this negative attention from strangers. I just can't believe the nerve of people.

TS present itself in many forms and it's not usually swearing! TS is an inability to filter your speech or actions. Tics are involuntary and senseless sounds and motions. Sometimes it is truly a curse, such as when we have to shoulder the abusive language and poor behavior from strangers. I've had a glimpse at the ugly side of humanity. Sometimes it's a blessing because I can empathize with other people in a way I might not have been able to if I did not have this disorder. I have also seen how wonderful people can be.

It took a few years of weekly talk therapy sessions and forcing myself to talk about my TS openly and to be okay with having TS, but I'm glad I reached this level. It took strengthening my spiritual life to fully accept that there is no cure and this isn't going away. It's not a cures or something to be mad at God about, it's just something different about me. It's changed my perspective on life. Now I feel it's my responsibility to be honest and educate those who are unfamiliar with TS. I might be the only version of TS someone will ever meet. My strength gives me back some control in regards to people's perception of me. I want them to know I have TS and not to believe their own assumptions or what they have been told by the media. If someone makes a strange noise, or movement that doesn't seem right to you, they probably do have something going on and the appropriate way to deal with the situation is to quietly approach them and ask, "Are you OK?" Politeness goes a long way, as opposed to screaming at them in public and demeaning them and their behavior. Don't make your own assumptions. As for me, I am a pretty normal-looking and well-functioning individual. I don't look like I came out of a cave and was raised by bears, so don't treat me like that.

Sarah 13

"I have no idea what I'm doing"

I'm thirty-six-year-old Sarah from Gainesville, Florida. Compared to other people's stories, I feel as my TS was a late bloomer. I didn't start noticing my first tics until high school, and wasn't officially diagnosed until I was thirty-one years old.

My symptoms weren't really noticeable in elementary school. I did have terrible anxiety in the form of shyness. I was bullied a lot and made to feel my lack of confidence was my fault. The school was really not much help, but we also didn't know what was wrong at the time. School didn't really get better for me until I started high school and joined the drama department and started performing in school plays.

I was picked on a little bit in high school, but it didn't bother me, as I was kind of laughing at my eye blinking myself. My tics came on first in high school, however, my father told me he noticed my eye blinking in elementary school. I didn't notice it until high school, during band class. It was very frustrating, and scary. One day in band class, I was playing my flute when I unexpectedly noticed that my eyes began to blink. Every time I would play my flute, my eyes started blinking, and every time I would stop playing, they would stop blinking. It felt weird, but also frustrating because it made it hard to read the notes. It became more noticeable to my friends in the band. When their section wasn't playing, they would notice my eyes blinking and would start laughing. They said, "What are you doing?" I was actually laughing at myself and told them, "I have no idea. I'm not controlling it. Can you help me!" We would all laugh. It was just weird to me.

I didn't have a computer or access to the Internet at the time, but I did go to the library and look up "eye blinking." The information that I got was of people with problems with their eyes, such as contact lens wearers and allergies, but I didn't wear contact lenses and I knew it wasn't allergies because it would only happen when I was play the flute.

About a month later, I noticed that I would make noises with my throat and the eye blinking was more persistent even when I wasn't playing the flute. My tics would become more pronounced, I would make swallowing noises with my throat and nose twitching. At the time, one of my friends asked me, "What are you doing?" I again told her, "I don't know." She said I should go to a doctor, but I told her I wasn't sure they could help. She said, "You could get a pill for it." I asked her, "Do you know what I have?" She said no, and I replied, "Then how do you know a doctor or pill would help?" Also around that time, I noticed if I would walk a lot, I would have so much trouble going to bed because of my legs kicking. Once I was in bed, I would just feel so restless. I didn't put the two together. In college, I thought I had restless leg syndrome because I felt, well, "restless."

I continued ticcing on through my adulthood. Eventually I got a job as a medical transcriptionist. My tics became very prominent at work, so my coworkers were very much aware. My tics were so severe at work that I would scream and say words that didn't make any sense. I would have tics that were so severe. It felt like I was possessed. I would punch walls, jump, scream, and use profanity. I also grabbed on to people and would writhe on the floor. I was already on Paxil, which my primary care physician prescribed for me for panic attacks. I told my coworkers I had Tourette syndrome even though I didn't have an official diagnosis. My coprolalia also began at work. I was lucky to have a little office, although, you could still hear the screaming outside the door. I tried putting towels down on the floor that I would get from the nurses. Everyone, including me, knew that these symptoms were TS, but we were also worried that it could be something else, like a brain tumor or some other neurological problem. My coworkers were very kind. One woman would come in and massage my hands as I was lying on the floor or she would massage my back if I happened to be lying on my stomach.

All this time I was trying to make an appointment to see a neurologist. It was taking forever to get an appointment. Finally, one of my coworkers stood by my side and told the neurologist's office that my tics were out of control and that I needed to get in NOW. They finally squeezed me in and the neurologist who examined me gave me the diagnosis of Tourette syndrome. I was actually relieved to get a diagnosis finally even though I knew I had TS. I was prescribed Catapres and Klonopin, to help with the tic, but it wasn't much help.

Along with my tics, I deal with the basic underlying issues that accompany TS. I have OCD, panic attacks, and depression. My OCDs are not that bad but I deal with some. Every time I throw out any type of bottle, it has to be upright. If it ends up upside down, I have to pick it out of the garbage and make sure it is straight up I just like to have everything in order. I will even go through the whole garbage and make sure everything is sitting straight up. I also have a cleaning OCD in my bathroom. I was worried about black mold in my soap dish, so I threw it out and bought a new one.

My depression is much worse than my OCDs. My depression comes and goes and can last for weeks at a time. Sometimes I think it will never end, and it just makes me feel sick. I wake up and feel like crying. I'm on a bunch of meds for my TS and depression, but I'm not sure if they are working or working well with each other.

Over the years, many of my tics have diminished, but I still do have a lot, and have developed new ones. I recently developed a new tic where I spit. I feel the saliva rising in my mouth and I need to be rid of it and spit in the trash, or sink. When I'm outside, I spit on the street. When I'm inside, I try to suppress this tic as much as I can, because I know I will have to clean it up. I'm not too verbal anymore, but I have noticed after bowel movements that my tics come on strong. I will get a bit vocal after that and scream "fuck," my hut tic, and a lot of body tensing. Besides that, on a normal day, I still have my everyday tics; ankle twirling, leg moving, facial grimacing, and especially at night, the kicking and nose twitching comes on. I pretty much have all kinds of tics, but I'm surprised when I start a new tic like the spitting tic. I wonder sometimes how far this will go. Will I start a tic where I inappropriately touch myself in public, or shout racial slurs? Just thinking of that scares me to death.

I start ticcing as soon as I wake up; actually, I sometimes wake myself up because of my tics. It can be 4:00 a.m. and I wake myself kicking so severely and or rolling back and forth. Usually I just wake up and start my nose twitching and mild eye blinking. I am currently on Neurontin for my tics, which it helps the symptoms but does not control them. Whenever I'm stressed out, my tics usually come out more. It usually comes out as coprolalia, screaming, or vocal tics. When I do feel nervous or feel my tics becoming more severe, I up my dosage even though my doctor has told me not to do that.

The hospital I was working at had to release me because of lack of funding in my particular unit. Several women of authority gave me an exit interview. I asked if this had anything to do with my TS. They told me that it didn't, but it still had me worried. They did make sure I could get a transcription job in another area of the hospital. Then I overheard my boss say to the other women, "I thought only boys had Tourette syndrome." The other women looked at her very uncomfortably. It was a very jerky comment that she made, and it hurt me.

My insurance ran out and I haven't been to a neurologist in a while. I ended up having to quit my job as transcriptionist because it became to stress full. It stressed me out so bad my tics became unbearable. So, now with no insurance and no doctor, I have been getting my medications from my primary care physician. However, I participated in a gene study and learned about a neurologist who I am going to start seeing soon. She is on maternity leave right now, but as soon as she is back, I'm going to try to get in with her.

Having TS is hard; I can't hold a full-time job. Right now, I'm working as an in-store demonstrator and still trying to pursue my dream as an actor. I love driving to auditions, film shoots, and I love acting. As for the in-store demonstrator, I still do get my vocal tics, but I try to hold them in as much as I can and let them out as whispers. I have to take longer-than-usual breaks.

I have noticed that with my period there are very little or no tics at all, then, all of a sudden, I get a tic explosion. I don't understand this TS. It waxes and wanes and you never know what's next. I try to stay active. I find the more active I am the less I tic. I try to read uplifting stories, and I pray. This all helps with my tics at times. I also will have a drink on occasion, as I find it helps me to relax, but when the effects of the alcohol wear off, I feel more nervous and sometimes have a huge outbreak of tics.

Exercise is a big thing too. I haven't worked out in a while, but I have noticed it diminishes my tics. I recently won a free gym class from a 5k-9 that I did with my dog, Bella. There was also recently a body and beauty expo in town and I won thirty free days of karate class. I'm excited to start working out again and maybe get a routine started, but I'm also worried because I take Catapres. Catapres lowers the blood pressure and if I do too much cardio, I start to black out. I hope that with more exercise, I will be able to build up my endurance. These are things that help, but if I'm depressed, I don't feel like doing anything and then my tics come out full-blown with coprolalia, screaming, etc. I'm excited to try this out, and maybe get back into a workout routine.

Right now, I'm on many medications. I am on Paxil, Klonopin, Catapres, and Neurontin. They work to control my anxiety level because if my anxiety rises, so do my tics. I feel like there could be some better medicines out there. Sometimes I don't take the prescribed dose and even exceed the doses I'm instructed to take. I worry about overdosing sometimes. When I take extra meds for my symptoms, I am so tired. In addition, when I am more tired, I become more depressed. When I double up on my Catapres, my blood pressure drops and I feel as if I am going to faint.

The medications help to a point, but I also have to watch my triggers. There are some things that trigger my anxiety and tics. Some

I can try to avoid, but most I can't. I think one of my main triggers is stress. Work also brings on many of my tics. I get angry when I have to go to work. When I'm in the parking lot, I start spitting and whispering profanities under my breath. The tics come on at certain times, like when I'm tired during the day or under a lot of stress. I know when I'm more tired because I am more severely ticcing. Also, that damn period. When I'm starting to get off my period, my hormones are crazy and so are my tics. Those hormones are a killer!

It's somewhat funny how this TS thing works. I'm also an actor and I'm trying to save up enough money to move out to Los Angeles. I visited out there, and it was so beautiful. I don't know if it was the change in environment or just the relaxation, but I didn't have a single tic when I was out there. At least not that I remember. I can't wait to get out there and pursue my acting career further.

I hope that kids and adults with TS will feel that they are not alone and that they will be able to recognize their symptoms of what I call "I have no idea what I'm doing" as possible TS or tics. I actually had no clue what I had and never knew what TS was until I was much older and in college. In addition, I want to make parents aware of these symptoms so they don't scold their children for doing them. My parents never scolded me, but I would tell them what I was experiencing and even though they were nurses, they still did not understand what they were. My mom actually never noticed my eye blinking—even though I had told her about it—until she was recovering from her hysterectomy in the hospital. She was even laughing and said, "Your eyes are blinking so fast." I said, "Finally, you see them. I don't know what it is..."

I'm very open about my TS. I have to be because people ask me, "Why do you do that?" I want to tell them why. It's not an easy life, but it could be worse. I feel like I am possessed when I have my tics, but at the same time, I am not quick to judge a person. I am very sensitive to people, especially their emotions, and like to talk to people if they are feeling depressed or having bad thoughts. I don't consider my TS to be a disease. I want to pray for other people who have Tourette and I wouldn't mind some prayers either. I have to maintain a strong faith in God, because I can talk to Him when other people don't listen. And even if He doesn't respond back verbally, he sends signs sometimes, usually things that make me happy, like casting calls and auditions or a beautiful dream. I have complete trust in God. I actually don't pray to be cured, I pray for my friends and family and people I haven't yet met. I feel God loves me and blesses me. I don't feel that He gave me Tourette to suffer. I believe that God doesn't send us suffering; He sends us peace. Lack of peace stems from the devil. However, even though I feel that I am suffering, I can offer it up to God as penance for nonbelievers or people who are in worse conditions than I am.

Richard 14

"A fighting world"

I'm Rich, well I'm not rich, but my name is. I'm a thirty-six-year-old man originally from Long Island, NY. I currently reside in upstate New York with my wife and stepdaughter, but I am in the process of finding a place in the city. Moving is hard, and it's hard to find a place that I am comfortable with. I know it's more expensive in the city, but I feel I can push my career forward in the city. I'm a musician. I play, teach, build, and repair guitars.

I guess I forgot to mention that I also have Tourette syndrome, along with ADHD, anxiety disorder, and rage disorder, but OCD is my big thing. I can remember having OCD thoughts as early as four or five years old. I was always worried about diseases, like cancer and HIV and contamination. There was a point in the 1980s when there was a tainted Tylenol scare, which from then on I associated any white pills with cancer. I soon became afraid to eat out of fear of being poisoned. The OCD about germs and disease caused a lot of anxiety and stress. It was so bad that when I was about five or six, I had such horrible stomach pains that I went to the doctor and found out I had gas caused by anxiety.

Because of my OCD, it took me a long time to get ready for bed. I used to go to bed dressed for school, because it would take me too long to get ready with all of my OCD rituals. Around that same age, I had to wear a retainer to bed, one of those horrible mouth contraptions. One time I was getting ready for bed and I dropped the retainer in the bathroom and it went sliding behind the toilet. That was it; it was done. Four hundred dollars down the drain. There was no way I was going to put that germ infested thing back in my mouth. My mother tried washing it and said, "See, its fine." I looked at her and said, "NO! Throw it away." My TS was not cheap for my parents. For a long time, I had a tic that I had to kick my toe into the street. I did it so much I would put a hole through my sneaker and sock and stubbed my toe until it bled. My parents spent so much money on shoes. They had to buy me a new pair every couple of weeks.

The OCD was very present before the tics even surfaced. The first tic I can remember was a spitting tic. It had nothing to do with my OCD, it was as if you were "Pssting" someone but with a spit. I would do this so much my mouth would dry out. This tic has stuck with me through the years.

When I was about twelve years old, I was driving my motor bike and crashed it into a car. After the trauma of the accident, I noticed the arm tic starting. I would throw my arm out to stretch my elbow. After that, the tics started getting worse and more tics surfaced. I started twitching my head, blinking, repeating words, grunting, throat clearing, a hmm tic, and a hut tic. Most of my classmates didn't really understand me while all of this started happening. They thought I was crazy, on drugs, or dangerous. In seventh grade, I had two kids who tried to bully me because they didn't know what was wrong with me or what I had. At this point, I still didn't know what I had yet. I remember having one of the kids come up to me, after months of bullying and torture, he said with such sincerity, "If you tell me why you do that, I'll leave you alone." The only way for me to stop the torturing was to give him an answer, but I had no answer. I guess I understand why some people have a hard time accepting me; I even had a hard time accepting myself for a long time.

At thirteen of fourteen, a little over a year after my tic started surfacing, I was diagnosed with TS. This is also when the second generation of tics started, the toe tapping tic. I still do it occasionally but for the most part, it's gone. They say tics run in cycles, I guess that's what it is. I went through dozens of pairs of shoes. Just imagine how many times you have to tap your shoe to actually put a hole through the shoe, then through the sock, and actually cause bleeding. I would walk, stop, tap, walk, stop, tap, and just repeat.

I had many issues trying to accept that I had TS. I denied it for a while. I hated the word "Tourette," It still does bother me in a very small way. Initially I blamed my father; he was the one that I got along with the least, so it just made sense to me to put the blame on him. I thought for some reason he was causing me to tic. It made sense to me at the time. I just had issues with acceptance, and openness. I didn't tell too many of my classmate, but my close friends knew. We would occasionally joke about it, and imitate my tics in a fun way, but of course deep down inside it took a toll on my emotions. As for everyone else, after a while, I didn't care who looked at me or what they thought. I didn't have the energy or passion to train or educate.

I moved to Florida when I was fifteen and it was one of the worst things that ever happened to me. I went from fancy Long Island, to the west coast of Florida, in the middle of nowhere. It was just a very different planet to me, but my father retired. I remember shortly after we moved, I was flipping through the yellow pages and came across an ad that read, "Did you move from NJ or NY and are suffering from culture shock? You're not the only one. Call for therapy." I grabbed the ad and showed my parents. "See, I'm not the only one. It's not just me. A lot of people feel the same way I'm feeling," I said. "I want to get out of here. I want to go home. I want to go back to New York." It didn't help that my OCDs and tics were getting a lot worse during this time. I had such a hard time moving to a new area, with new people and dealing with my TS. This just meant I had to do a lot more explaining to new people.

I did become friends with a kid right across the street from me, I mean directly across the street from me. I give him a lot of credit. With my tics, my OCDs, and even my anxiety getting worse, he was very accepting of me. There would be times when I was over at his house and I had to go home to go to bed, but I couldn't cross the street. I developed an OCD where I couldn't cross the street because I couldn't touch the little white dots on the road. When it was time to go, I would just go into panic attack mode, so he would carry me piggyback across the street. As soon as I got across the street, I would run to my front door, and yell back, "Thanks, man." He would just reply, "No problem." It amazes me to this day that this person would do this for me, and I wonder what went through his mind. I don't know if I didn't have TS if I would be able to do something like that for someone... I always wonder if he did it out of friendship or sympathy. Either way, I give him a lot of credit.

Not everyone is so accepting, especially in school. There was not much understanding or even help from my teachers. I had one teacher put me against the chalkboard and surround me with easels and boxed me in so I wouldn't bother or be bothered by any of the other students. She would also put my desk in the hallway. The school got to a point where they thought the best thing for me was to put me in a resource class with special ed. and learning disabilities. Besides having tics, and OCD, this did not help with my relationships with my fellow classmates. It just gave them more stuff to bully me about. There was one time there was an open class for the parents to observe the class, and my mother came. I had this thing where I had to lean back in my chair, I'm not sure if it was an OCD thing, or a tic, but I always had to do it. I was doing it during the open class and I fell back and landed on the floor. My teacher looked at me and told me to stay on the floor. I stayed on the floor the rest of the day. Not only was I humiliated, but also so was my mother, but in these times the teacher was always right, the principle was always right, and the doctors were always right. They never wanted to listen to my mother, or even cared to understand. Finally, my mother set up a meeting with my school principle, teachers, and an advocate from the TSA. This still didn't do much good, they just refused to care, or understand. It was shortly after this, that there was another meeting with my mother and the school psychologist. She told my mother, "I can get your son to stop ticcing. It's ridiculous. I can get him to stop ticcing in an hour." This was not the way to approach the situation with a Sicilian mother; she went ballistic. I ended up quitting school in the tenth grade, got my GED, and went to college.

When I was around eighteen or nineteen, my OCD plagued me to a point that my mother bought me a book, *Brian Lock* by Jeffery M. Schwartz. She constantly tried getting me to read it, but I didn't want anything to do with it. I had dealt with so many doctors, and I didn't want another one telling me how I was supposed to feel. I didn't think anything that they had to say would help me. They didn't know what I was going through, or how I felt. My mother would leave the book on my bed every night, and I would walk in and throw it on the floor. One day my OCDs were so bad and the book sitting there. I was feeling desperate, so picked the book up and looked at the back cover. There was a picture of a brain before and after reading the book. This gave me creditable evidence. I started reading the book and following the steps and felt like it started working right away. The theory behind the book is changing the brain chemistry by changing your thoughts. I was just so excited that it helped me. It didn't get rid of all of my OCD thoughts, but it helped much more than any of the other things we had tried over the years. My parents had tried quite a few methods for my OCDs. I remember doing behavior therapy, where I put dryer lint in my shirt and wore it around, exposing myself to the irritant, the obsession. Nothing helped except this book.

As I entered adulthood, I stopped hiding my tics. It became more difficult to hide them, and plus if I was out, I didn't enjoy my time if I was focusing on hiding them; I would just rather tic. When I was twenty, I was with my girlfriend and a friend at a restaurant. I was ticcing a lot, and the person at the table behind us made some nasty remarks. I don't even remember exactly what he said, but for some reason my tics were annoying him. It was strange. I had never dealt with a reaction like this before. I'm usually more on the aggressive side, but I think I was just shocked and embarrassed. I was also shocked that my friend didn't come to my defense either, but my girlfriend did. My girlfriend looked at him and said, "My boyfriend has Tourette syndrome." I was so embarrassed, I guess I wanted her to yell out "Fuck you!" not scream out to the whole restaurant that I have TS. The guy just ended up muttering under his breath and the night went on.

I had a great group of friends who were very understanding. A few years ago, I found a bunch of old answering machine tapes from the medication day. I would easily sleep for fifteen hours at a time, and my friends would get worried. They would call every hour saying, "Rich, its ten o'clock. Wake up. Rich, its 11:00. Rich, it's twelve. Rich, it's one. Okay, Rich, it's two. We're coming over!" They would come over, wake me up, and get me out of bed. It amazes me all the years and years I missed out, now I'm playing catch up. I missed so much of my life just being a zombie and emotionless. I could have won a million dollars, but I would just sit there thinking, "I know I'm supposed to be happy or excited, but I can't feel." I guess that's the way it is with antidepressants. They make you numb to the world and your surroundings. I was on so many medications that made me very lazy and lethargic that I spent most of my time sleeping and being very inactive. In about three years, I gained so much weight and reached 265 pounds, which is a lot for my small-framed body. I grew tired of all of the side effects of the medications and weaned myself off them against my doctor's wishes. I figured I would rather deal with myself without the side effects; I felt like I was missing out on my life. I started walking and then doing a little exercise and lost a hundred pounds in eleven months. In addition, I thought exercising would help some of my tics. I didn't help, but it helped release energy. I needed to feed the stimulation.

I guess with my OCD, I just feel medications are like poison. I went to a doctor a few years ago and I told him I had been on medications since I was thirteen. He was trying to figure out what medication I had been on and which ones I had not taken. He asked me to make a list so he could figure out a new combination. I made the list and gave it to him. It had fifty-two different meds on it. He was speechless; he thought I was joking. I explained I wasn't.

I think my grandmother had TS, but was never diagnosed. She passed away when she was ninety-six and never believed she had TS, even after I was diagnosed. My mother said to her, "See, Mom, you have the same thing as Richard. You have TS." She would just say, "No, I don't.," but she always told me, "I have to take my nerve pill (Valium)." She started ticcing when she was a kid, after seeing her father killed. They were driving a got a flat tire. Her father went to change the flat tire and was hit by a passing car. When it happened, my grandmother jerked her head away as to not see him. This became one of her tics, then alterations of it. She would always joke about not being able to wear long earring, or getting whiplash. She had other tics, like grunting, and the hut tic. When no one was around, or she thought no one was around, she would have very loud vocal tics. In the 1920s, she actually had shock treatment, but I'm not sure if it helped her.

As for now, most of my tics are gone, or at least decreased. They started decreasing after my twenties. Now I'm just plagued with anxiety, OCD, and a few tics. My arm tic went away for a long time, but I've noticed it has recently started to come back. I still do the spitting tic, and now because I try to suppress my tics I have started a jaw-clenching tic. I guess I internalize a lot more than before. My tics have subsided to a point that most people don't even know I have TS, sometimes I don't even know I have it, but I am very conscious of my anxiety and OCDs. Sometimes I feel so exhausted just being awake that I feel like I'm fifty or sixty years old. It clouds my mind with so many thoughts and I tend to lose focus very easily. I start a project and never finish. I always pride myself on having a photographic memory, but I find myself forgetting more as the years go by. Now I find myself making lists of things that seem endless.

I can suppress my tics, but I can't suppress my anxiety, and OCDs. It feels like I'm in a constant battle between my physical and mental state fighting my anxiety. My body is consumed with fighting the anxiety, and it's hard to find enjoyment. I'm always in my own world, a fighting world. When it comes to being social, I have to prepare myself, get out of my own world, and join the social world, but once I do, I am still engulfed in my own anxiety and thoughts—a thousand thoughts a second. It's a challenge. I consider myself a very social person. I love being social, but when I'm done, I feel so exhausted, violated. At the end of the day, I just try to unwind, which really is not a word in my vocabulary. I don't watch too much TV, but I love to listen to music, practice on my guitar, or watch YouTube videos. I rarely drink, but I think it relieves my TS symptoms for a short while.

Even though I suppress my tics when I'm out, I still try to stay true to myself about my TS. I might not offer the information to someone, but if they ask, I am open about it, especially when I was in the dating scene. I was always hiding my tics for the first couple dates, but was open after that, and told the girl that I had TS. They said, "I thought so," or thought that I had some nervous thing. I thought I was hiding the tics, but I guess not. I never felt any discrimination; they actually thought it was cute. That wasn't always the case with their parents. I remember I had one father that did not like me or the fact that I had TS. He told his daughter, "Don't bring that TS kid in my house, and don't even think about marrying him." When I met my now-wife, I wasn't too worried about having the conversation. Her sister has Down's syndrome, so I knew there wouldn't be any prejudice.

About six months ago, I was doing some research online about TS and found the NYC chapter of the TSA. I e-mailed the chairperson and after a couple conversations, she invited me to her summerhouse to meet her and her family. She had a daughter in her twenties with TS. It was weird for me because this was the first person I had met who also had TS. I was thirty-six years old and had never met anyone else with TS. It was like looking in the mirror; we were so similar and had many of the same tics. After that, I started getting more involved with the TSA. I started going to different events and meeting more people like me.

When I was younger, I thought I was normal, and then this thing happened. This "problem" that made me do weird things that I couldn't explain or understand. It wasn't until my later years that I realized what a blessing/curse TS is—I actually named my music production company Blessing/Curse.

People with TS are similar, but different. I'm insecure and immature, it's just part of my personality, and I love it. I love that after thirty-six years I have found others like me, that understand me and what I'm going through, people that I relate to.

Above anything, I guess I just want people to see someone with TS for who they are and not what they do. When you see someone twitching, making a noise or being different, don't judge him or her or consider him or her crazy. It's a symptom of a disorder and that's all it is. You're not discriminatory against someone with diabetes. I have TS, but it doesn't define me. You should really try to embrace them. You will find that we are an amazing group of individuals, and you'll never be bored.

Michael 15

"Talking about it was my life saver"

My name is Michael. Originally, I am from Syracuse, NY. I am now living in Brooklyn, NY with my wife and three-month-old daughter. I'm the campaign director for the American Cancer Society; I coordinate all of their political advocacy efforts in New York. I'm thirty-seven years old and was diagnosed with Tourette syndrome at the age of nine.

When I was eight years old, my parents first noticed me making funny faces and doing things with my mouth. I would open my mouth as wide as I could. My mother would say, "Stop. Why are you doing that?" I told her I couldn't help it, and she just replied, "Of course you can help it!" It's not that the tics that bothered me as much as it was that they interfered with my daily life. When I was reading or playing sports, I would twitch and people would ask me what I was doing or tell me to stop. I would say, "How? I can't help it." They would just roll their eyes at me as if I was being a troublemaker or yell at me. In time, my parents realized that I really couldn't stop, and then they started to get worried.

Around the same time, I started having problems in school. I was in class and I would close my eyes and bend my neck down toward the desk as a tic. The teacher thought I was falling asleep and would tell me to wake up. I told her, "I can't help it." She yelled at me for this and sent me to the principal's office on many occasions. I started to struggle in school and with things that I normally loved to do, like playing sports and reading. My parents started getting desperate, so they finally took me to our pediatrician. The pediatrician looked at me and said I might have Tourette syndrome and we should go to a neurologist. My parents were shocked. "Oh, my God, my child is not perfect."

It was not really a struggle to come to terms with my TS, but it was incredibly hard to handle as a kid. Some kids would make fun of me, but most just said okay and went back to playing or whatever else they were doing. For the most part, kids in my grade were good to me. They knew me, and I was friends with most of them. They understood that my tics were not my fault; therefore, they did not tease me. The kids in the class above me on the other hand regularly teased me. They would mock me behind my back and to my face. They gave me nicknames and called me out in public. They never even considered if it bothered me. After my diagnosis, some parents were mean and would not let their kids play with me anymore, but most were fine.

While I never struggled to come to terms with it, I did struggle to understand it. As a kid, I went through bouts of depression. I had a bad eye-blinking twitch, and I would struggle to keep my eyes open, in school. I would twitch so much all day long that it would just leave me physically exhausted by the time I got home from school. I would often come home, curl up on the sofa with my dog, and just cry, but happy that my dog didn't think I was weird. As I got a little older, I started to find humor in my twitches as a way of laughing off any teasing. Soon I was coming up with nicknames for all of my twitches. The nicknames made me laugh, others laugh, and that made dealing with them easier. From that point forward, I used laughter and communication as my main tool for dealing with my twitches.

When I was ten, the doctors put me on Haldol. The side effects were bad. They knocked me out, slowed down my metabolism, and increased my appetite. I was a happy-go-lucky ten-year-old boy, energetic, healthy, thin, and friendly. All of a sudden, it all changed. I started falling asleep all the time, even in the middle of dinner. I was always starving, gaining sixty pounds in two years. Now I was the chunky, overweight, sloppy-looking kid who made funny faces, weird noises, and kicked people. I went from a kid with many friends, to a kid who was shunned and teased by everyone.

In fifth grade, I was on the school bus on my way home, and there was a mentally challenged seventh grader on the bus. He saw me making faces and thought I was making fun of him. Out of nowhere, he just came up and punched me in my face. I ended up getting a black eye. It was sort of a tricky situation because of his own disabilities, as he had no ability to distinguish between what I was doing and what he thought I was doing. There was also an incident in eighth grade. I was on a ski trip and I had a girl smack me across the face because she thought I was winking and hitting on her. I had no idea what was going on. It happens a lot with kids. A twitch can cause confusion with kids.

My parents were both very supportive. They were both committed to helping me, getting me help, and being patient with me. I started seeing a child psychologist. It was comforting. When I saw him, I would talk about my TS and my twitches. By talking about it, it made me stronger. The more I talked to him, the more comfortable I felt talking about my TS. As a result, by the time I was twelve, I was telling everyone who would listen. I told them about my TS and explained it to them. I talked to teachers, students, and anyone who would listen. Suddenly I wasn't strange; I didn't have this strange condition that no one knew about. I was just Michael. Talking about it was my lifesaver. It actually wasn't frightening for me, because I have always been a very outspoken person. I was never shy. As I got older, I would struggle to figure out the best time to tell people, but once I did, I had no problem explaining it.

I am a very slow reader. After growing up dealing with severe eye blinking and other twitches, it was so tough for me to read as a child. As a result, I never really developed a love for reading, and I never became a quick reader, which put me behind in school. Still to this day, I am a very slow reader, which has often made school and work challenging. I just read at a slow pace because I constantly blinking my eyes. I would squeeze my eyes so tight I would give myself a headache, over and over again and rubbing my eyes. All my eye tics and bobbing my head made it hard to read. We would get books and textbooks on tape, but this was hard. This was in the 1980s, so I would order the tapes for the assignment and it would take six to eight weeks to get the tapes delivered. By this time, the assignment was already due. My mother would end up having to read the book to me. It was not like reading to your toddler, she was reading eighth-grade curriculum. In class, the teacher would always give us the "take thirty minutes and read to yourself in class and we'll discuss it after" assignments. It was a pointless exercise for me. They would be done it fifteen minutes, and forty-five minutes later, I was still trying to finish. I tested with a relatively high IQ, above the majority of the class, but it was still a struggle. It finally was recognized and I was allowed longer time. I still have trouble, but I listen to NPR news and many different podcasts to get the information that I enjoy. For my work, I need to read many newspapers and follow the news in detail on a daily basis. My TS has made it incredibly difficult to read and my work very challenging.

I have relatively minor levels of OCD; it's not severe, or limiting in any way. For the most part, I need to have stuff put away and cannot live in a cluttered environment. I need to put everything away before I go to bed at all times. At work, I need to file and put away everything before I can leave at the end of the day. As a kid, I had many little things that I had to do before I could go to sleep and on a nightly basis, I would have obsessive thoughts run through my head over and over again.

Many of my twitches start first thing in the morning, such as facial movements, head bobbing, and arm movements. I try to do a lot of stretching, because it sort of helps prevent the tension. The brain wakes up, and so do the tics. I usually start the mornings off the same. I wake up and take me dog and my three-month-old daughter for a walk through the park. It's usually a good walk, but I find myself stopping and stretching a lot. One thing I have noticed over the years is that my tics are worse in the summer, when it's hot and muggy.

When we get home from our walk, I'm tired but I still have to get ready for work. At this point, most people would have a coffee, but not me. Caffeine is generally the worst thing I can do for my tics. If I drink a cup a coffee, within minutes I can feel my TS getting worse. I feel the tension building up in my blood stream and spreading through my body. A horrendous feeling of tension and twitches.

I pass up the coffee, and begin the task of getting dressed, which is a whole other problem. I have to dress up for work, wearing a suit, slacks, and a tie. The tie is the issue, I have a problem with restriction, especially around my neck, and it sets off tics. I usually don't button the top button on the shirt and leave the tie slightly loose as to avoid too much restriction. Many of my tics come out through my neck, and if anything pulls, restricts, or touches my neck, it will trigger more tics throughout the day. If I have a tight-fitting shirt, it will drive me insane all day and I will have to tic. I always have to put a lot of consideration into what I'm wearing as not to aggravate my TS.

I think one of the most difficult aspects of my day would be my train ride to work. It's a thirty-minute train ride, thirty minutes of everyone desperately trying not to look at one another, while at the same time everyone is trying to stare at everyone. The first thing I do is find a place to stand where I will have room to twitch; I have to have room. If the train is packed, my TS will go through the roof. If I'm next to anyone, even in a car and we have to touch, it will make me want to twitch. For holiday dinners, I have to sit at the head of the table because I can't sit between people; I can't be crammed in. I do everything in my head, from counting sheep to singing to distract myself until I can get off the train.

All my tics in my face are a little crazy. I have eyebrow twitches, blinking, and tongue tics. I can suppress my arms, legs, and head on the train, but everyone can see my face. There's nothing I can do. I look around and see people staring and looking at me and occasionally making fun of me. I actually had this little boy staring at me one time, I was twitching like crazy, and his staring just frustrated me more and more. It wasn't his fault, but he was driving me nuts, but I deal with things like this every day.

The train ride home at the end of the day is not much better, it's actually worse. There are more people and I'm tired after a long day of work and suppression. I just try to ride it out. I listen to my iPod and try to lose focus. I am comforted by the thought that I will be home soon, and I can get out of the restricting clothes, and not have to suppress my twitches anymore. I get home, and get into loose-fitting clothes. It helps me helps me out because ultimately what I want is to not twitch anymore, but I still get home and have a huge tic attack. Sometimes I'll have a beer or a gin and tonic, one is usually just enough to take the edge off and calm my muscles down. If I have more than one drink, my twitching will get worse.

Going to sleep at the end of the night can be frustrating. It's hard to sleep. I'd like to hold my wife and fall asleep, but that's just not possible, because once again, the feeling of restriction. I have to sleep with my back to her, because I'm likely to hit or kick her with my twitching. I twitch so much within that first hour and often twitch throughout the night, which then leads to a bad night's sleep, leaving me tired and groggy in the morning.

The biggest way that my TS has changed over the years is how I dealt with my twitches and how different tics came and went. As a child, I took Haldol, which made me fall asleep all the time. As I got older, I tried various medications before finally landing on Clonidine. I have been taking Clonidine since I was eighteen, which has been working relatively well for me. In addition to the meds, I have learned to get lots of rest, do lots of stretching, and even some yoga helps. Finding ways to relax is crucial. I love music, listening to it, dancing to it, and just about anything with music relaxes me. I also try to maintain healthy eating habits and limit my sugar intake. I have seen over the years that sugar can set me off, and just a bad diet will trigger more twitches. I just try to do all the little things that help me calm my twitches.

I have a three-month-old daughter and I can't help but look at her when she wiggles and hope she doesn't develop TS. My TS has made me the person I am today, and I'm proud of who I am. I may have some hang-ups, or be self-conscious, but I'm happy with who I am. I'm comfortable. I credit my TS for making me the person I am; the compassionate person who has spent his entire life fighting for other people with TS. If I had a chance to do it all over again, I would not want to have TS. But there is no question that it has made me who I am, and I'm proud of that. I do feel I have something special to offer because of my experiences. There are people with TS that are a thousand times worse than I am.

I feel like my TS is a bit of a curse, but overall it has been a blessing. I would not wish it on anyone, but it has indeed made me a better and stronger person and I am proud of who I am. Sometimes I feel physically worn down, but I still keep a positive attitude. I am very open about my TS. I have been speaking publicly about it since I was twelve years old. It's important to remember, although TS will be a challenge, it is a challenge that you can overcome. The key is to learn to talk about it and communicate about your tics. Become your own biggest champion. Being able to explain your condition will be a tremendous asset throughout your life. Lastly, learn to laugh about your tics. If you can find humor in your tics, you will be better off. As a child, I came up with nicknames for my various tics. There was the chicken, the Jesus, the Fred Astaire, the spider, and others. These allowed me to relieve the stress of my TS in even the toughest times.

Steve 16

"I wish I knew then what I know now"

My name is Steve. I'm an IT system administrator from Toronto, Canada. I'm now thirty-eight years old, but was originally diagnosed with Tourette syndrome when I was about twelve years old. I can trace my first tics back to when I was nine years old. I might have had tics earlier, but I wasn't aware of them at the time. The first tic that I can remember was a licking tic. I would lick my upper lip, and outside skin until it was raw. This tic came and went, and no one could explain why. If there were more tics, no one noticed or said anything about it.

Before I was diagnosed, life was confusing. I was a happy twelve-year-old boy and I just didn't understand what was happening to me. When I was around eleven years old, the tics became more noticeable. My friends would say a lot of things like, "Stop doing that," "Why are you doing that?" or "You're doing that again." Sometimes I wasn't even aware that I was doing it, or simply couldn't explain that I couldn't stop. No one could explain it. My parents took me to doctors, and they had no clue. I tried my best not to do it. I thought it was as if I could stop, but I didn't know that at the time. I just kept trying to stop, and just thought I was going crazy. "Why can't I stop this?"

After all the doctors, the way we discovered I had TS was through a friend of my brother. My brother's best friend had TS, and was diagnosed much younger. He was over one day and we were all hanging out. I did one of my tics and he noticed. He turned to my brother and asked, "How long has Steven been doing that for?" My brother said, "Been a while I guess. Why?" The friend said, "He has Tourette syndrome." I immediately turned around and said, "What is that? What does that mean?" It was a funny sounding name, somewhat scary, but exciting. There was a reason I was doing this, and someone else was doing it too.

My parents called his parents and got their doctor's number. We made an appointment, and by the time we got to the appointment, I was scared half to death. I didn't know what this TS thing was. You hear names of diseases and think death. I had a big fear that I was going to die from this TS thing. The doctor looked at me for about ten minutes and said, "What you have is Tourette syndrome." He explained it and put some of my fears to rest. I was happy there was a reason I was doing this and I wasn't going crazy.

I was actually not too upset at the time. Suddenly I had an explanation as to why I was doing these things, these tics. All this time I thought I was going crazy, but now I had this magic pill that seemed to make my tics pretty much go away. The doctor put me on Haldol and at least one other medication, which I cannot remember the specifics of. The Haldol reduced my tics quite substantially but caused drowsiness, which was the reason a second was tried. The second medication had virtually no effect at all, on neither my tics or my side effects. The pills made me sleepy, but it was generally better than the alternative. For the first time in a while, I felt a little normal. The tics had been getting pretty bad, and it was nice to feel normal again.

I know maybe it's a little weird, but telling my classmates was not an issue. I guess maybe because I had been in school with the same group of kids for almost six years. Suddenly I could explain that there was a reason why I could not stop doing those things I was doing. I remember being excited to go to school to tell them and explain it. At first, it seemed okay. It was in the start of the seventh grade that things began to change. The anxiety and depression began, which made my tics worse.

As I headed toward thirteen years old, the tics got worse and anxiety kicked in, which made tics even worse. Friends started closing me off. They never really said anything; they just stopped talking to me. At first, they just ignored my tics, and then they started to ignore me. I was left with one friend who stuck by me. I'm not sure if he wanted to stick by my or just felt he had to. He was okay with it. Mostly he seemed to try and not pay attention to them. I eventually did make a few friends, and did feel that the friendships were genuine.

If I was having a bad tic day, I had permission to go to the nurse to calm down or go out of the school setting. I would go to a friend's house who gave me a key to his house. He would check if I was all right to go back to school. A lot of time I would stay and sleep, relax and eventually go back to school, or go home. I had a few friends that didn't judge me. Sure, it had some impact on them. It had to at that age. I was just thankful to have friends.

There were kids I met in junior high, who never knew me without TS and were the "not-so-cool but nice kids." They seemed to accept me. There were also the kids who bullied me a bit. Not so many though. There were good times and bad times with my fellow students, as well as the bullying. At this point in my tics, I had a barking tic that made me an easy target for bullies. Kids would mimic me. There was one point that sticks in my head; it's burned in my memory. I was having a reasonably good day when I walked into my eighth grade shop class and all the kids simultaneously mimicked my barking tic. It was a very defining moment. I turned around and ran out. I hid in the bathroom embarrassed and crying. It was one of the most painful moments of my life.

After that incident, I didn't want to deal with school anymore. I just couldn't deal with the stress. The public school never tried with me. I felt as if they just tried to sweep me under the rug, and that I was the sore thumb sticking out. They didn't want to deal with me and gave me very little support. There were individual teachers and administrators who tried, but there was still not adequate support.

This is also the time the depression kicked in; there's only so much a kid of that age could take. I was admitted into the hospital for suicidal thoughts. When I got out, I lost touch with my friends and I never left the house, or my room. I didn't want to feel this way anymore, I just wanted to get better and I didn't know how. The following school year, ninth grade, I ended up missing so much school that they tried to get me to start tenth in basic classes. There were three levels of class, advanced, general, and basic. I refused to start the tenth grade in basic. Up until this point, I was in advanced classes. I wanted to redo the ninth grade in private school. It ended up being the breaking point, which my parents pulled me from the public school system and put me into a private school. I ended up attending the private high school for two years. They worked closely with me so that I could succeed despite my challenges, and I did.

That summer I went to an overnight camp. Things were getting bad for me. A friend found me alone. He had noticed I was always sad, depressed, and ticcing. He asked me what was wrong and I explained it to him the best I could. He told me that he suffered from serious depression. He pulled out his Walkman and said, "Here, listen to this." It was the song "Never Surrender" by Corey Hart. When I was done listening to it, I was in tears. He said nothing about that, but took the cassette from the Walkman and gave it to me and said, "Here, keep it." Then, in an unusual moment for two fourteen-year-old boys, he just gave me a hug. After that, I never went anywhere without that cassette. It was with me for years. The whole song helped me out a lot, but one specific part that really helped:

And when the night is cold and dark
You can see, you can see light
'Cause no one can take away your right
To fight and never surrender.

When the summer was over, I went on to my first year at the new private school. Even though it was much more accommodating, I still dealt with issues attached to my TS. Besides my tics, I also had anxiety, panic attacks, anger disorder, and OCD. All of these underlying disorders were still unknown to me, but they were there. During that first year, I had a panic/anger attack when another kid accused me of taking his pencil. All the pencils looked the same, but I knew I didn't take his pencil. As soon as he accused me, I left the room to calm down. When I came back into the room, the boy had broken the pencil in half. That was it; I flipped out. It was a complete brain meltdown, out of nowhere. I left the room again. As I was out, I remembered that because of my unknown OCD, I always had six pencils with me. In case anything happened to the first five pencils, I always had a sixth. They were always ready for use. I went back in the classroom and pulled out one of the five pencils left, this really pissed off the other boy.

I was never actually diagnosed with anger disorder, but I do feel it in the depths of me. There have been different occasions where I just could not control my temper. There was one time I pushed a friend into a wall just for touching me. I just got so upset that I would be on the verge of tears. I'm a big video game player and after a kind of anger fit, I now make sure to have something soft next to me when I'm playing any game, so if I get upset and throw something, it will be soft and not break anything.

I spent two years in the private school before reentering the public school system. By this point, my tics were pretty much under control. By the time I was eighteen years old, my TS had pretty much disappeared. It got very mild, so I thought the medications that I was still on were unneeded, and I weaned myself off them. My TS just went on a steady decline to a very manageable low.

There are two chapters to my life with TS: TS as a kid, and TS as an adult. As a kid, I tried to reinvent myself, tried having tough skin. I spent my childhood trying to pretend that I was like everyone else, but I think everyone with TS tries this. We're not like everyone else. I spent many years not even thinking about it. I was just trying to get by in a world where I felt as if I was the only one with TS. I soon became okay with myself, accepted myself. A lot of my depression was not accepting myself. I pay more attention to my TS now than I did as a kid. When I was a kid, it was something more that my parents had to deal with, but now that I'm an adult, I have to deal with it.

After my TS faded, I spent many years denying it altogether until its recent reemergence. After twenty plus years with TS, I have now finally come to terms and accepted it as part of who I am, and in some respects, I take pride in having TS. Most of my adult life, my tics were very manageable and under control. My tics pretty much disappeared until a couple years ago. I went away with friends for a weekend. We had a great time, nice and relaxing. About two weeks after that, my stomach tic started again, then another one and another one, then the eye tics. I didn't get it. I didn't understand what was going on. This wasn't supposed to happen. It mostly went away, and here it is again.

I have good days and bad days. I just need to make sure to get enough sleep. I used to be able to deal with five to six hours of sleep, but now I need to have my seven hours of sleep, or I'm too ticcy and stressed. I need my sleep. When I don't get sleep, my tics get worse, and then my anxiety gets worse, which triggers more tics. It's a big TS snowball effect. I have noticed that my tics are more apparent in the morning and at night. The tics start as soon as I get in the shower. I think I actually tic in my sleep, because there have been times that I have woke up with scratches on my left cheek.

I stick to patterns in my life; I'm a very ritualistic. This helps me keep my tics in check, but they still affect me on a daily basis. Sometimes they go away, sometimes new ones appear. A few months ago, I started a throat clearing and cough thing. At first, I thought it was a cold, but I have concluded that it's actually a new tic. New or old you learn to adapt. Different ones can be distracting, like my eye roll tic and foot tic. It's hard to drive while my food has a mind of its own, or my eyes are rolling and blinking. I just have to be extra cautious.

My TS is something that I always notice. As an adult, my family, friends, and coworkers don't seem to notice, or they just don't care. On occasion, my closest friends will make lighthearted jokes about my tics, but I have given the permission to do so. They don't make fun of me, they are just funny about it and it prevents me from taking myself too seriously. They make me laugh, and I actually enjoy it. It's better than me sitting around saying, "Why me!"

Along with my tic, I also have OCD, anxiety disorder, and likely, ADHD. I have the attention span of a ferret. I'm always like, "Ooohhh, look at that shiny thing." I have never officially been diagnosed with any of these, but I just know it's part of TS, and I know it's there. My parents always called me a creature of habit, but it's really just my OCD. I tend to do many things the same way every time, especially my morning routine, it is always the same way every day. My OCD is just very patterned, and I like to think I have kept it under control. It never really bothered me, I just like to have things a certain way, and very organized. I guess the organization part can annoy someone else, but I'm fine with it. I have a DVD collection of over seven hundred that always needs to be in alphabetical order.

I try to keep my TS under control as much as I can. I try to stay relaxed and do calming things. I know that stress and fatigue triggers my tics. I go to the chiropractor, which was originally for a back issue but I have now found helps reduce my tics. After a long day, I like to watch TV, movies, play video games, or just hang out with friends. I know I don't have to suppress my tic in front of my friends, so I never feel anxiety about that. I might have a light drink because it seems to calm my tics down, but too much makes my tics go crazy. It's all about finding what keeps me calm.

I was never allowed to use my TS as an excuse, and so I never really think about it stopping me. I'm very open about it now, and I talk about it. My TS is part of me. It's what I am, who I am, and I like that. Would I be "me" without my TS? No, I'd be a completely different person, and I like who I am. My TS has never stopped me from doing what I want and I've never let it stop me from trying. TS is part of me, but it isn't all that there is to me. Kids survive cancer; I can survive this.

Roy 17

"This is my gift"

My name is Roy. I'm a forty-three-year-old actor/producer living in NYC. I'm also a co-owner of a production company. Originally, I'm from Long Island, NY. It wasn't a far move to the city, especially to pursue a career in acting. Oh yeah, and I have Tourette syndrome. I hate saying that; the word just made me cringe.

I was originally diagnosed at eleven years old, but I started exhibiting repeated blinking at around age six. About a year later, I started what I thought was a habit of stretching my mouth. I later realized this was a tic. This turned into a troublesome tic, causing cracking of the jaw and fever blisters in the corner of my mouth. My mother had a conversation with my second grade teacher about these new peculiar habits. My teacher just felt it was something I did when I was nervous and not something to worry about. She just thought it wasn't anything that was disruptive or cause for alarm. At the time, I wasn't too aware or even self-conscious about these tics.

The first time it was brought to my attention was when my parents sat me down to talk to me about these nervous habits. They just wanted to know if I knew I was having these nervous tendencies, and if I could control them. I told them that it was just something I had to do, and I couldn't control them. Now the self-conscious feeling had started because the fact was it was brought to my attention.

Soon after this, I started exhibiting some other tics like head jerking, grunting noises (almost like barking), and a few others. This is the point where friends started noticing. My friends started asking questions, but since I had no idea why I was doing these things, the questions embarrassed me and I just made up some excuses or ignored them.

By the time I was in fifth grade and diagnosed, my TS was something I tried to keep to myself, especially since my tics were fairly mild. If someone did ask me about a tic, I would just brush it off as a nervous habit that I had, no big deal. If it reached a point where someone actually asked me if I had TS, aside from feeling embarrassed, I would secretly be angry, as if they found me out. All that went through my head is, "What do they know about TS anyways!" The truth is they probably knew as much as I did. I needed to educate myself more, but I was too afraid. The word "Tourette" made me cringe, especially being that it was a syndrome. It brought on a lot of embarrassment. I was used to having these tics, and I felt like, "Why do I have this condition with such a weird name like Tourette syndrome."

Right after I was diagnosed, I started seeing a psychiatrist who tried to help me by experimenting with medications. I was on Haldol for a while, which made me feel sluggish and depressed. I was falling asleep every day at the same time in my social studies class. I would rest my head on the desk and just go to sleep. No one ever said anything about it; they just let me sleep. After talking to the doctor, I was then prescribed Cogentin to mitigate the side effects. I eventually had no zest for life and my mom didn't hesitate to take me off the medications. I didn't start taking medications again until I was in my late twenties and I sought out the help of a New York neurologist, who prescribed me Clonazepam. I've been taking that ever since.

Besides falling asleep, I didn't have that much trouble in school. I had a lot of friends; I was a very social person. The friends I had were great, and they never said much about my tics if they noticed them. There were times where someone would say in a joking way, "Do you have Tourette or something?" I would just blow it off. I never said I did. I was really just hiding from the fact. Even teachers made comments from time to time. My throat tic would always raise questions, not about TS, but about being sick. My teachers would always ask if I was sick, and I would always say yes because I was embarrassed to go into why I was doing what I was doing. I had an incident with my seventh grade teacher once when I was having a bad neck day with my tics. In front of the whole class, my teacher asked me if I was trying to give myself whiplash. I was mortified, but I think I genuinely surprised her and caught her off guard because she didn't know that I had TS.

I never had too much mocking or judgment due to my TS, but I did feel it for someone else one time. When I was in eighth grade and was making my confirmation, there was another boy who had TS. I didn't know him, he was just there with us, but I noticed his tics. He had a lot of noises and vocal tics. I remember during the rehearsal that he was exceptionally loud. Being so young, I remember feeling bad for him, but also being relieved I didn't have it that bad, or like that. I guess it also made me realize that it could be worse.

I think when most people think of Tourette syndrome they imagine people who curse uncontrollably. That's never been something I've done. For the most part my tics have been consistent. The tics have waxed and waned over the years. All of the tics that I have experienced throughout the years include eye blinking, mouth stretching, throat clearing, clicking, tensing my shoulders, head tossing, jerking my right arm, slamming my elbow into my side, and a lot of neck tics. I also have some rare vocal tics where I make a chirping sound, a sound like a puppy whining noise. I hurt myself ticcing, and I get really soar from the neck cracking. There was even one time when I threw my arm out, smashed it into the microwave tray, and scratched the skin on my knuckles. It was both annoying and kind of funny. I have recently started a new tic, which scares me. I have started slamming my head forward, to the point I feel like my brain is bouncing around in my skull. It really freaks me out. I always wonder if I am damaging myself.

Along with the tic caused by TS, I have my share of underlying disorders. Although I was never diagnosed, I know I have anxiety disorder and I guess I consider myself OCD to a point. It's not a counting or germ type of OCD, but I definitely have a cleaning compulsion. When I'm working, I find myself cleaning and organizing my workspace before I can actually work. I need things to be in order before I can move to another task. Once everything is neat and clean, I feel my brain is neat and clean and can start working. I just love to clean, I mean really clean. I feel more relaxed and in control of my life when my environment is clean and orderly. I can be somewhat of a perfectionist with a love and attention to detail, which I consider a great benefit as an artist. However, the compulsion to get things clean and orderly before taking on greater tasks can be somewhat of a hindrance and what can feel like an endless loop cycle.

It's hard to discern between the physiological and psychological. The tics are something I just deal with and control as needed, but the need for organization is harder to deal with. I function best when my schedule is very regimented, but being my own boss, that can be quite a task. I feel like it's a huge benefit because I am constantly putting myself to the test every day. Sometimes I think my life would be easier on some level if I had a job where I punched a clock. When I was in college, I took a job on an assembly line making skylights, but my creative side was screaming to get out. Personally, I need to find the balance of order and regiment with excitement and adventure.

I think this all falls into a bit of the anxiety too. I have a lot of anxiety about getting everything done that I need to accomplish in my life, yet I always feel I'm on first base. I feel like I'm always starting at the beginning. Maybe it's just a symptom of living in NYC, or an effect of my OCD. I just worry about not reaching the level of success that I dream about in my career because at some point people will find out that I have TS.

I'm not really on medications for my TS, but I am prescribed Clonazepam for the anxiety. My doctor thought that if I calmed the anxiety down that the tics might do the same. I can't really say if it's working because I don't actually take it as prescribed. The prescription is to take one .5mg pill three times a day. I've been prescribed this for years but have yet to actually try three pills a day. It rather scares me to take that much. One reason is that I know you can build up a tolerance to it and they would just keep upping the dosage. I usually take one pill before bed, and on occasion, I might take one in the afternoon if I'm really stressed. I will take a pill if I know I'm going to be performing on stage or on film. On occasion, I think it might be interesting to take the three pills a day just to see how much it does help with my tics, but I am just worried about building up a tolerance. I often wonder if I've already built up a tolerance, but it does still take the edge off.

There are other ways I try to deal with the stress. For instance, at night I like to take a bath to try to unwind. I also found watching TV or reading can help too. I generally find that I'm particularly fidgety and ticcy when I sit down to read, but it subsides after a while. Listening to music is also relaxing at times, but lately my life is extremely busy and I don't find much time to relax or unwind. Sometimes I might have a drink to calm myself down. I have found drinking affects me differently depending on the time or environment. Sometimes it can make me more ticcy, sometimes not at all.

I've never been one for drugs, but I have smoked marijuana. I believe it actually makes me less ticcy, but it wasn't something I really paid much attention to at that point. My true vise is caffeine. I'm sure it affects me but I never tried to do anything to test the effects if I stopped. I'm sure I'd be less ticcy but I just need that morning pick me up, and throughout the day too. I used to drink a lot of coffee in college, but don't know how aware I was of my tics at the time. I have never felt compelled to stop drinking coffee. I guess it might be beneficial to stop, but now it's just normal to me.

I've never thought of having TS as a struggle, it's just something I deal with, but I guess it's a struggle in the sense that I spent most of my life in denial. I didn't acknowledge it or discuss it openly or freely. It was just something that I dealt with but ignored. I know that even with TS I can accomplish anything I put my mind to—well, I'm not going to attempt tightrope walking, but I don't think there is anything I can't do if I really want. I just need to keep in mind to be more open.

I know that spending so many years with my TS closed has not been beneficial. About eight years ago, I was at the gym and a guy noticed me ticcing. He approached me and asked if I had TS. I was surprised, because I always felt like I hide my tics well. I guess not as well as I thought. I was so freaked out, as if I had been outed. The guy was sweet and sincere in the way he approached me and explained he also had TS. He was just trying to help and tell me about the organization. He gave me his card. I really thought I was going to follow up with him but I didn't. I had a lot of reservations, and I also lost his card. I regret now not following up with him, but I just wasn't open to this part of my life yet.

A similar situation happen to me a few months ago in October 2011. In the morning, I like to do a Buddhist ritual chanting. This particular morning I was chanting about work, future, and success in both. A thought of my TS popped in my head, and I briefly thought about trying to find out more about TS, and finding some information on the TSA (Tourette Syndrome Association). This was weird that this popped in my head, because I was still in the closet and denial about my TS, but I started thinking how my neglecting my TS was affecting my career. If I didn't acknowledge it or embrace my TS, how will it further hinder me? I ended the thought with thinking, "I should Google it someday," and I continued chanting on about my career.

About five hours later, I was walking my dog, and I went a route that I very rarely took. As I was walking past a storefront, this guy came running out and stopped me. He very nicely introduced himself as Troye Evers and asked me if I had TS. I looked at him and finally with openness said, "Yes, I do." We talked for a few minutes. He openly discussed his own TS and his involvement with the TSA. He told me about a biography that he was working on about a bunch of people with TS and asked me if I might be interested in being part of it. It was weird; everything that I was chanting about just a few hours earlier was right in front of my face.

From that point on, I started being more open. I was finally becoming comfortable in my own skin. I started talking about my TS more. I had done a one eighty. Meeting Troye has helped me open up to a completely new world, and friends. I now go to different events and I am meeting more people like me, people that I can relate to and that relate to me. I'm sure that on a subconscious level I thought of having TS as a curse, but now I'm determined to turn that belief around into a blessing and a source for reaching out to help others.

We all have a range of tics and disorders, but unlike the media portrayal, not everyone with TS has a debilitating case. For the most part, we can overcome and lead a normal life. There are many people afflicted with TS, but we are all human and just like everyone else. We can hold jobs and function in society. I no longer feel sorry for myself. The more you become accepting of yourself, the more others will be accepting of you. Whatever your challenge is in life, it's your gift. This is my gift.

About the Author

Troye Evers was born in the suburbs of Chicago to Edward and Donna Evers. It was a very troubling and difficult childhood dealing with divorce, strict parenting, and many behavioral issues. Even though his tics started around ten years of age, he was not officially diagnosed until he was eighteen. After years of daily teasing and being made fun of at school, he learned to try to control the tics and hide them as well as he possibly could. He hid his tics, resulting in him hiding from himself. He rarely spoke of his Tourette syndrome, or his tics, and often made up excuses for his tics, as many children do. "My throat is dry," or, "I slept on my neck wrong."

Troye has always had a passion for writing, mainly screen and TV writing, but after being removed from his junior year high school English class and put into a learning disability English program, he developed a fear of following his dream. He continued on the path of hiding, hiding his tics, hiding his writing, and hiding from himself.

At the age of thirty-two, he started coming out of his shell and began revealing his writing, but still remained in the "TS closet." It wasn't until he wrote his second screenplay, *Tic*, that he came out of his shell and stopped hiding. Writing this screenplay, he learned a lot about himself and his TS. This script went on to win third place in the 2009 All Access Screenwriting competition. A couple years later, he was voted onto the board of directors for the Tourette Syndrome Association's New York City chapter.

In his struggle to raise awareness for TS, Troye decided to move away from screenwriting. He came up with the idea to write a one-time blog article documenting a day in his life with TS. Within a few days of posting the article, he received over a thousand hits and had numerous comments requesting more. This is when the screen-writer turned to author and *A Day in the Life of Tourette syndrome* was born.

A Day in the Life of Tourette Syndrome

By Troye Evers

September 21, 2011

Tourette syndrome is a neurological disorder characterized by repetitive, involuntary movements (tics) and vocalizations. As a writer and a sufferer of TS, I decided that I really wanted everyone to know what a day in the life of someone suffering from TS is like.

Many people with Tourette syndrome differ in many ways, as in the tics they have and what underlying conditions accompany their Tourette. Besides my tics, I also have anxiety disorder and obsessive compulsive disorder. Frankly, I wish I were void of the anxiety disorder. With the anxiety disorder, I feel like a roller coaster, the tics trigger the anxiety, and the anxiety triggers the tics. My tics are very mild, but very frequent. Most people don't even realize I have Tourette syndrome until I tell them, but even on a good day, I tic at least every ten seconds. (I have a neck and shoulder tic, and a throat-clearing tic.) This is a twenty-four-hour study of my life with TS.

Good morning. It's 6:53 a.m. and here I am, another day, another tic. Sometimes I think there is something wrong with me. I don't have to be at work until noon, so there is no reason for me to be up this early, but like usual, my internal clock has said, "Wake up!" There's no sleeping in for me. I lie in bed for about ten minutes before the anxiety hits and I have to get up. All I can think about are all the things that I need to do today, all the things I need to do before work.

Without even thinking, I get up, get dressed, and grab the dogs. It's time for our morning walk, and a chance for me to grab my coffee. I've lived in my neighborhood for four years and I'm very familiar with my neighbors, but I pray that I can make this walk without being bothered. My main goal is to get back home and get started on my already growing list of things to do. I just hope to get safely back into my house where I don't have to worry about anyone seeing my tics.

I make it home unbothered. As soon as I get home, it is time to start cleaning the apartment. My husband thinks this is ridiculous, seeing our cleaning lady is coming today, but there are things that she doesn't do, and won't do. I guess that in reality, I just want to set up for her. Yep, call me crazy but this is just the beginning. First thing I do is sanitize my hands after walking the dogs. I feed and water the cats and dogs and sanitize once more. Now for the dirty job of cleaning the cat pan. I sanitize about three times in this process. I'm sure glad I started extreme couponing, now I have about twenty bottles of sanitizer that I paid only $1.00 for each, normally costing $3.49, but that's beside the point. I continue doing little things around the apartment.

Now it's time for me to get ready for work, and I'm stressed about time. I need to make sure I am out of the apartment by 10:00. My cleaning woman usually comes around 10:30, and if I'm there while she is, I will just end up following her around telling her how to clean. "Why don't you dust like this," or "Wouldn't it be better if you used this attachment for the vacuum," etc. I have found it's just easier for her, and me, if I leave before she gets there. I finish getting ready and 10:00 approaches. I'm struggling to get out of the house.

Along with my other disorders, I think I have a bit of agoraphobia. I'm most comfortable at home, but I know I have to leave. I keep on finding little things around the house to do. Finally, around ten after ten, I hit a point of frustration where I just grab my bag. I double-check that I have my hand sanitizer and mini Lysol. I grab my keys and run out the door.

On my one-block walk to the subway, I put on my sunglasses and earphones. This makes me feel like I'm in my own protective bubble, well, protected to a point. I guess it really just makes me feel blocked from the world. Every morning I have such anxiety getting on the train, "the human germ sardine can." I am always able to get a seat on my way to work, but that's not usually the case on my way home. It's much easier if I can sit and not actually have to touch anything with my hands, although if I am standing, I always have my handy dandy handkerchief to hold onto something. I have found there is always ways around not touching things in public. I can usually use a public restroom hands free. I lift the toilet seat, flush, and depending on the restroom, turn on the faucet with my foot.

Once I'm actually on the train, my anxiety grows, and so do my tics. I try everything to calm them down. Every morning I wish I had taken a Klonopin before I left. My mind runs away with things that I need to do, so I pull out my phone and go to my notes app. The daily list fills up fast, usually with nonsense but stuff that I don't want to forget. I count down the remaining stops until I get to my stop. I don't know why, but on the train, I just feel so vulnerable. Through my dark-tinted sunglasses, I see people looking at me. I sit and wonder, "Are they looking at me because they've seen me tic, or is it just the fact that I'm covered in tattoos?" I guess with all the tattoos I've really just asked to be stared at, but for crying out loud, stop! At least with my headphones on, I can mask my neck tic as a possible little dance to my music.

I finally reach my stop. I always try to make sure I'm the first one out. It's like a break for freedom, rushing up the stairs to fresh air. I arrive at work. Once again, I'm the first one there and left to wait for someone to get there with the keys. I sit on the sidewalk in front of the salon and wait. The only thing that goes through my head is, "Do the passing cars see my tics? Are there people in the apartment building across the way staring at me out their window?"

The receptionist shows up and unlocks the doors. I'm semi-comfortable in the salon; everyone knows I have TS, so I never have to explain myself. Don't get me wrong, if someone approached me on the street and politely asked me what was wrong with my neck, or if they offered me a cough drop, I would have no problem saying I have TS. It's the people who don't say anything and just talk and snicker that bother me. Most of my clients know I have TS. Strangely, I have no problem touching people's hair all day, just don't touch my hands. It can get somewhat hard with new clients when they come in and shake hands and then they see me sanitize right afterward.

Every day I dread going home. About half of the time I break down and take a cab because I know the train will be so packed, more so than when I came to work. Now it is the tail end of rush hour and I know I will end up standing. Just the thought of holding on to the handrail in the train makes me want to sanitize while I'm writing this (honestly, I just did.) Even with taking a cab my tics are bad. I see the cab driver continuously looking in his rearview mirror at me. My husband and I have a car, but still I usually refuse to drive. When I'm driving, my neck tics are really bad and I'm afraid I might cause an accident, so for the safety of other people on the road and myself, I stick to the subway or cabs unless it is a very short distance.

For the sake of this study, I do take the subway, and of course, I am left to stand. I grab my handkerchief out of my bag and hold on to the handrail. All I can think of is that they have done studies where they have taken swab samples of the handrails in the subways. They've found E. coli and feces (sorry, need to sanitize again). I continue holding on and just try to meditate to calm my tics until I get home. As always, I'm the first one out of the train so I can make my break for the fresh air and freedom.

Once I get to my building, I slowly start relaxing. Since I have been trying to hold my tics back for so long on the train, as soon as I get in the elevator I snap like a rubber band. It is a violent looking tic. As soon as I'm done I always look up at that little corner mirror that they have in elevators. I wonder and hope there is not a camera behind there. It's a horrifying thought that someone could be witnessing my display of relief.

The first thing I do when I get into my apartment is to start fixing all the things that my cleaning lady has moved. The garbage can in the bedroom, the end tables next to the bed, the way she makes the bed, the shower doors, something on the bookshelf in the hallway, etc. It's the same things every week. There's a place for everything and everything has a place, and I will know if it is moved even an inch. It drives me nuts, but I deal. When I'm done rearranging things, I can finally relax. I grab a drink, and if my husband is home, he will have dinner ready, or close to it. Otherwise, I will start cooking. The rest of the night is usually a nice, quiet evening of just watching TV. I'm in the comfort of my home and I can finally chill out. I can comfortably tic without any judgment. About thirty minutes before bed, I take my Klonopin to help me fall asleep. It just helps my mind not obsess while I'm trying to fall asleep.

In all actuality, this was a good day for me. Some days are worse than others are. I don't want anyone reading this to think I am complaining at all. I just really want to let people know what it is like in the shoes of someone with TS. I have a great life, two jobs that I love doing, a great support system of friends and family, and most of all, a great loving husband. Like I've said earlier, my tics are on the mild side of the scale. There are a lot of people out there suffering a lot more than I do, especially children. No matter what, I love my life and I live it one tic at a time.

Made in the USA
Middletown, DE
21 February 2017